O9-CFS-819

Twayne's English Author Series

Sylvia E. Bowman, *Editor*

INDIANA UNIVERSITY

John Cleveland

TEAS 180

Vera et viva Effigies Iohannis Cleeveland.

Photo courtesy of Yale University

John Cleveland

By LEE A. JACOBUS

The University of Connecticut

TWAYNE PUBLISHERS
A DIVISION OF G.K. HALL & CO., BOSTON

Copyright © 1975 by G. K. Hall & Co.

All Rights Reserved

Library of Congress Cataloging in Publication Data

Jacobus, Lee A
   John Cleveland.

   (Twayne's English authors series; TEAS 180)
   Bibliography: p. 158–59.
   Includes index.
   1. Cleveland, John, 1613–1658.
   PR3348.C7Z7   821.4   74-26734
   ISBN 0-8057-1095-7

PR
3348
.C7Z7

MANUFACTURED IN THE UNITED STATES OF AMERICA

66785

For French R. Fogle
and J. Max Patrick

Contents

About the Author

Lee A. Jacobus teaches Milton, Shakespeare, and Modern Irish Literature at the University of Connecticut. His books include *Sudden Apprehension: Aspects of Knowledge in Paradise Lost* (Mouton: The Hague, 1975), *The Humanities Through the Arts*, with F. David Martin (McGraw-Hill: New York, 1975), *Aesthetics and the Arts* (McGraw-Hill: New York, 1968), and other texts for use in colleges. His articles have appeared in *The Huntington Library Quarterly*, *The Bucknell Review*, and *Milton Studies*. His poetry and short fiction have appeared in such magazines as *The Southwest Review*, *The Carolina Quarterly*, *New Mexico Quarterly* and many others. Currently he is at work on a book on Shakespeare.

Preface

John Cleveland was almost certainly the most popular English poet
of the 1640s; but most of those who know his name today have
learned in the brief footnotes of seventeenth-century poetry an-
thologies that Cleveland is a decadent poet who wrote in a worn-out
mode; he was too extreme in his use of metaphysical wit; and he was
not able to control his material. Cleveland is spurned as the last of
the Metaphysical poets and as a probable incompetent. Even his
kindest critics treat him with a deference that suggests an ultimate
distaste for him. This book offers a reassessment and a close reading
of his work; and, as the first book-length study of the poet, it is long
overdue.

My feelings about Cleveland are that he was a shrewd, sensitive,
and highly intelligent poet whose greatest strength was his knowledge of his audience. When we think of the primary strain of
Metaphysical poets, we think of those who wrote for a small, courtly
audience, such as John Donne, or those who wrote at times for an
audience of one, such as George Herbert. None of the early
Metaphysical poets were poets of the people, or poets whose work
would have widespread currency and relevance for the readers of
their time. Cleveland, on the other hand, depended on the kind of
audience attracted to the new political newspapers ("mercuries," as
they were called): a partisan, volatile audience quick to rage and
quick to adulation. His prose made him the darling of these readers,
and their affection demanded numerous editions of his poetry,
much of which was about political subjects in a satiric style precisely
suited to the tastes of the time.

Because of Cleveland's ability to satisfy so completely the readers
of his own day, the readers of later times have found him sometimes
difficult, sometimes obtuse, and sometimes incomprehensible. In
any case, they have found little to respond to and much to recoil

from largely because the modern reader not only has little detailed information about the political, religious, and social circumstances of 1640s, but he also is virtually uninvolved in the enormously passionate disputes of the day, disputes Cleveland delightedly joined. In other words, some of the problem of appreciating Cleveland is the problem of topicality. Like most topical poets, Cleveland faded as his audience's attentions were drawn to new problems. But the fact is that Cleveland's genius was real, and it is well worth reconstructing the historical circumstances which make possible a good reading of the poetry. Much of my effort in succeeding pages is to show that, when we understand Cleveland's references, we can understand his poetry. Perhaps it is ironic that the more successful a satirist is, the more necessary such reconstruction is if later eras are to appreciate his achievement.

Another reason we may avoid the work of Cleveland is our prejudice against rhetorical poetry. Cleveland's genius was a rhetorical genius, one that permitted him to turn his academic—but nonetheless public—talents as rhetoric reader at Cambridge to excellent use in the public forums of the entire nation. The same gifts that made him valuable to the university made him valuable to the general public; for, like most successful rhetoricians, Cleveland knew his audience and his audience's limits and expectations. A good rhetorician plays on these as a musician plays on an instrument: much of his technique of persuasion is calculated in terms of its ability to produce a specific response from the listener.

Even that which is outrageous is useful to the rhetorician—perhaps more useful to him than to anyone else. Cleveland's ability to turn his university gifts of rhetoric to good account in public life depended on his willingness to properly assess the nature of the public audience. As far as we know, he had no special background which might have suited him for doing so: he was not "a groundling," though perhaps his immediate circumstances as the son of a relatively impecunious minister aided him slightly. His success as a rhetorical poet also depended on his willingness to breech decorum and to say things he knew would be regarded as outrageous by some. He well knew that some of his audience would condemn him for such behavior and that a larger number would applaud him; but all would take notice of him.

The most outrageous technique Cleveland used was the Metaphysical conceit, the surprising yoking together of dissimilar things which, upon reflection, are seen to have important similarities. But Cleveland's use of the technique was so extreme that it earned its own name: the Clevelandism. John Dryden defined the term as "wresting and torturing a word into another meaning."[1] A good example which still annoys some readers is the phrase: "my penne's the spout/Where the rain-water of my eyes runs out" from "Upon the death of M. King drowned in the Irish Seas." The concept of his pen's being a rainspout for his tears is indeed extreme, recalling some of the almost embarrassing images of Richard Crashaw's religious poetry. But we realize Cleveland is simply telling us that, while others may express their grief with tears, he expresses it with his pen. Whatever the immediate shock of alarm and incredulity may be for us on first reading the line, we cannot deny that it demands our attention and gets it.

In these terms, Cleveland can be regarded as a poet influenced by the mannerism of poets like Richard Crashaw in English and like Giambattista Marino in Italian. Even John Donne indulged occasionally in poetry which took such careful aim at the sensibilities of the reader that it could be considered mannerist. All mannerist artists rely on shock value and on a keen awareness of the norms of expectation of their audience. However, not all mannerist works have quite the shocking effect that some of Cleveland's poems still have for us. The interesting thing is not that they shock us on the level of their subject matter or their attitudes toward direct address—as do the poems of Donne, Crashaw, Lord Rochester, and some others; instead it is Cleveland's technique that alarms us, his use of language and imagery. The modern reader finds the same lack of coherence and unity in some of Cleveland's poems that we find in some mannerist paintings, such as those of Pontormo, Parmigianino, Velasquez, and those painters who sometimes willfully distorted their subjects or introduced totally foreign figures and elements as a way of calling attention to their manner. Cleveland's manner is unquestionably striking; and, like some of the mannerist painters, he has been called to account on matters of technical capability. I feel he is unjustly brought to task because I see great care in his apparent disorganization and in his efforts to produce extreme effects in the mind of the reader. My feeling is that Cleveland is a psychological poet in the sense that he is constantly aware of the nature of his audience and is constantly concerned with maintaining an aesthetic pressure on the reader.

Such a feeling is by no means whimsical. The most recent scholarship about and criticism of the works of John Milton, Cleveland's almost exact contemporary, suggest that Milton's concern for his reader was such that it conditioned the structure of *Paradise Lost.* Since both Milton and Cleveland were educated on "the self-same hill," Christ's College, Cambridge, at the very same time, it should be no surprise to discover that the attention their studies gave to rhetoric should have made them both sensitive to the needs and the deficiencies of their audience.

The first two parts of Aristotelian rhetoric are invention and disposition. Invention is the finding of matter: the discovering of arguments or images or conceits to present to the audience; and disposition is the arranging of those invented matters. History has noted well that Cleveland was a most inventive poet: his conceits still stand alone, marking him, all by themselves, as a singular poet. But history has also condemned his invention as being too extreme. Cleveland's invention is said to be ultimately incoherent because each moment of invention—each Clevelandism, if need be—stands alone. His disposition of those moments, in other words, is said to be faulty. Instead of organizing them so that we proceed in orderly fashion from one dramatic conceit to the next—as is usual in the poems of Donne—we are jarred suddenly from one extreme moment to another.

I do not think the charge of incoherence holds up. It sounds very much like the arguments which would condemn Shakespeare for his puns or for his mixing of metaphors. It sounds, too, like the argument which would condemn picaresque or episodic novels for being nothing but a succession of high points with no organically integrating troughs between them. Cleveland's poetry is usually a succession of brilliantly invented high points, each of which demands and gets total attention from us. The end result is somewhat like that of the episodic novel: we are dazzled, breathless, and sometimes infuriated.

My reading of the poems concentrates, where necessary, on establishing the historical circumstances which have a bearing on the poems' meaning, but it concentrates even more on a close textual reading which demonstrates that Cleveland's work is not the product of haste and an unwillingness to revise, as some seventeenth-century specialists have felt. An analysis of Cleveland's prosody alone, such as that I begin with in chapter 2, should show immediately that Cleveland is cautious, calculating, and extraordinarily careful of the effects his poetry obtains from the reader. Once we agree that Cleveland may, indeed, be in control of his materials—an assumption we normally accord to the most obscure poets—we are then ready to apply some critical attention to the poems in an effort to see if they may not, after all, be worth reading carefully. My feeling is that they must be read carefully.

The first chapter of this book establishes what is known about Cleveland's life. We are indebted primarily to the researches of John Berdan, though the more recent researches of Samuel Vogt Gapp may have helped us understand something of Cleveland's life after the death of King Charles. Chapter 2, "Clevelandism," examines the technique that was graced by his name: the extreme mode of conceit in the Metaphysical manner. The effort of the chapter is to demonstrate that Cleveland's invention found a congruity between extremes of feeling and extremes of ingenuity. Readings of such poems as "The Hecatomb to his Mistresse," "Upon an Hermophrodite," "The Authour to his Hermophrodite," "A Young Man to an old Woman Courting him," and in particular, "Upon the death of M. King drowned in the Irish Seas," suggest that while we may, as moderns, question the extreme technique, it may have been exactly this technique that Cleveland's audience depended on for knowing Cleveland's true feelings about his subject.

"Cleveland's Lyric Voice," chapter 3, offers readings of calmer lyrics such as the two Mark Antony songs, curious essays of complementarity demonstrating the wit and ingenuity Cleveland put to different purposes in his satires. Many of these lyrics have the quality of an exercise designed to amuse a witty audience. Cleveland's poems of love also have some of that quality, including "To the State of Love, or, The Senses Festival," "The Antiplatonick," "To Julia to expedite her promise," and the famous "Fuscara; or The Bee Errant." Yet, they are fascinating poems and quite successful when they are closely examined. If they are exercises, they are exercises in reason and wit which still have the capacity to please the modern reader.

As chapter 4, "The Political Cleveland," suggests, Cleveland's muse was drawn into the lists to do political battle on the side of his king. The invention and elegance of the poems discussed in the first three chapters of this book gave Cleveland a weapon easily adaptable to the purposes of attacking his enemies and bolstering his friends. This chapter provides enough of the historical, religious, and political background so that the average reader can appreciate Cleveland's invention and his concerns. The principal poem treated in this chapter is the generally encomiastic "To P. Rupert," celebrating the Royalist hero, Prince Rupert, whose expertise and dash made a Royalist victory seem a certainty. But the political situation was remarkably complex, and the strange earlier poems "On the Archbishop of Canterbury" and the "Epitaph on the Earl of Strafford" show a very different—almost quiescent Cleveland. These poems reveal a range of feeling and a range of technique which is not revealed earlier.

Once the Royalist cause failed and the Commonwealth established Presbyterianism through the land, Cleveland turned almost exclusively to satire. Chapter 5, "The Satiric Strain," gives us Cleveland as the most vitriolic and effective satirist of his time. Perhaps he did not invent English satire—that satire which names names and attacks persons and institutions directly—but he must be considered the finest early practitioner of the mode. All of Cleveland's preparation in his lyric poems and his early political poems proved fruitful in his satires. His incredible invention, his ingenuity, and his capacity for pushing language to extremes make such poems as "A Dialogue between two Zealots, upon the &c. in the Oath," "Smetymnuus, or the Club-Divines," "The Mixt Assembly," and "The Rebell Scot" enormously rewarding. The success of such poems for the modern reader depends on an understanding of the situations and the conditions that impelled Cleveland to write in the first place. This chapter, in offering readings of the poems, supplies much of the necessary information for the general reader.

Chapter 6, on the prose, offers large sections of the prose, which has no modern edition, as well as some interpretation of Cleveland's work. The striking thing about the prose is that it depends heavily on the poetry for its techniques and for its references. And perhaps most important for us to realize is the fact that it was the prose that first made Cleveland a national figure. The samples we have are relatively few and relatively short, but they establish Cleveland as a formidable prose satirist in the best tradition of the seventeenth century.

The final chapter offers a brief history of criticism concerning Cleveland.

Preface

The attention Cleveland has received from critics in our century has been slight. Yet, we are indebted to John Berdan's edition, which includes a brief introduction and a number of useful appendixes informing us about the contents of seventeenth-century editions of Cleveland and which includes virtually all we really know about Cleveland's life. George Saintsbury's 1921 edition, in *Minor Poets of the Caroline Period*, adds very little to Berdan; but Saintsbury carps at Berdan as if he were a competitor instead of a colleague. The landmark edition of the poems, however, has only recently been made available to us by Brian Morris and Eleanor Withington, who established the canon of Cleveland's poems for the first time in their *The Poems of John Cleveland* (1967). Their work makes it possible for a meaningful, current assessment of Cleveland; and, though they do not, of course, give us specific access to the prose, every critic working with Cleveland is deeply in their debt.

Further indebtedness of mine must be mentioned. I would like to thank the William Andrews Clark Library for a summer grant and the use of its remarkable holdings in the literature of this period. The Henry E. Huntington Library, the Wilbur Cross Library, the Honnold Library, the Francis Bacon Library, the New York Public Library, The Beinecke Rare Book and Manuscript Room were all generous with their holdings. The University of Connecticut freed me for a summer with a faculty summer grant. I would also like to thank some friends, teachers, and colleagues who were good enough to listen to some of my ideas and to read some of this book in manuscript: J. Max Patrick, Christopher Grose, William Sheidley, Irving Cummings, and Raymond Anselment.

LEE A. JACOBUS

University of Connecticut
Storrs, Connecticut

Chronology

1613   John Cleveland was baptized at Loughborough on June 20; his father, Thomas, was a rural clergyman and grammar-school assistant, educated at St. John's College, Cambridge, B.A. 1608; mother, Elizabeth Hebbe, died 1649.

1621   Family moves to Hinckley; John educated by Richard Vines, later a member of the Westminster Assembly.

1627   September 4, admitted as lesser pensioner to Christ's College, Cambridge.

1629   Chosen to deliver Latin welcoming address to the Earl of Holland, Chancellor of the University.

1631   Takes his B.A.

1634   March 27, elected to the Hebblethwaite Fellowship in St. John's College, Cambridge.

1635   Takes M.A. From now to 1637 he is Rhetoric Reader.

1642   March, gives speech before King Charles I: warmly received; June is the last official mention of Cleveland at Cambridge.

1643   With King Charles's forces at the headquarters in Oxford.

1644   "The Character of a London Diurnal" published in two editions.

1645   May 27, appointed Judge Advocate at the garrison in Newark.

1646   May 5, King Charles surrenders to the Scots near Newark; on May 6 or 7, Cleveland surrenders Newark to the Scots Commander, David Leslie. For nearly ten years Cleveland virtually disappears from sight.

1647   *The Character of a London-Diurnall: With severall select Poems By the Same Authour*. Like the rest of the editions, doubtless printed without Cleveland's authority or permission. Five reprintings with additions in this year.

1651 *Poems by J.C. With Additions.* Nine editions of this title.
1655 November, consigned to Yarmouth prison for at least three months; there he wrote "To the Protector after long and vile Durance in Prison."
1657 Possibly at Gray's Inn practicing law.
1658 Thursday morning, April 29, dies of "an intermittent fever."

CHAPTER 1

"The Grand Malignant of Cambridge"

I Family and Schooling

JOHN Cleveland, who was born in central England in Loughborough, a small market town of Leicestershire,[1] was the son of Thomas Cleveland, the assistant to the rector of the parish church; and, a clergyman himself, he had John baptized in Loughborough on June 20, 1613. Thomas Cleveland was an educated man; he had received a B.A. from St. John's College, Cambridge, in 1608; and he held, in addition to his position at the church, one as an assistant schoolmaster, or usher, to John Dawson in Burton's Grammar School. John Berdan speculates in his biographical introduction that Thomas maintained his job as usher, which paid four pounds a year in two installments, in order to supplement his church income and to provide adequate support for his family. He did have eleven children between 1611 and 1633 (his wife, Elizabeth Hebbe, died in 1649), but not all of them survived. Two, Mary (b. 1611) and Thomas (b. 1618), died very young. One child, Thomas again, died at the age of nineteen, after having been admitted to Christ's College, Cambridge, only the year before.

The family fortune seems to have changed when, in 1621, Thomas managed to secure a living as vicar of Hinckley, also in Leicestershire and the home of his wife's family. From this time on, the family prospered considerably with the exception, of course, of the period of the Commonwealth, during which time Thomas, as a Royalist sympathiser, was repeatedly in danger of losing all his holdings. The king's troops lost a battle at Hinckley in 1644, and Parliament tried, up to the year of Thomas's death, 1652, to pry his land from him.[2] They also tried, apparently, to convince him to join their party, despite the fame his son John had already won as the chief satirist of the opposing side. Like his son, however, Thomas died loyal to the king.

One of the curiosities of life at Hinckley was the fact, recorded by some of Cleveland's early biographers as well as the register at Christs's, that John enrolled to study with one of the most prominent Puritan divines of the area, Mr. Richard Vines. Considering the importance of religion in the curriculum of the day, we wonder that Mr. Vines's views did not affect Cleveland more than they apparently did. Like his father—who may certainly have played a hand in keeping John true to the Church of England—John found Puritan opinions unsuitable for his own purposes. John's life at Hinckley may be considered to terminate with his enrollment in Christ's College, Cambridge, September 4, 1627.

When he went to Cambridge, John was fourteen, by no means unusually young, though the college records list him as having been fifteen—meaning that he was in his fifteenth year. The question of why John did not enroll in his father's college (none of Thomas's sons did) has been troublesome to Berdan and others; and, though there may be any number of reasons, we will never be in a position to know them. But one reason for John's choosing Christ's may have been his tutor, William Siddall. Siddall, second or third in order of seniority among the thirteen Fellows of the college, was himself a Leicestershire man and may have been known to Thomas, who was at St. John's just before Siddall (B.A. 1601) would have accepted a Fellowship.

Like Milton, and in Milton's own college, Cleveland was enrolled as a lesser pensioner and his fees were fifty pounds a year, a not inconsiderable sum at that time, particularly when we consider that Thomas had received a twelfth of that sum for teaching school only a few years before. As a lesser pensioner, John would have been entitled to the same privileges in the college that Milton enjoyed[3] and would have been a member of that middle grade of students. This rank was lower than that of the greater pensioners, or fellow commoners, who were often not very serious students, and who paid more of a fee and received more benefits from the college; and it was higher than the sizars, or poor students, who worked at odd jobs in the college and who sometimes shared rooms with the Fellows, or tutors, as a means of saving space and money.

Christ's was the third largest college at Cambridge in Cleveland's day, consisting of approximately 270 students and Fellows. Not all students lived in the same building—some were even surreptitiously boarded out—but most students probably knew of each other if they did not know one another well. The chances are that

Cleveland knew Milton, who had achieved recognition in Christ's as a poet, and it seems certain that they both knew Edward King, whose death in 1637 motivated each to write an elegiac poem. On that occasion Milton, of course, wrote *Lycidas;* Cleveland's effort was simply titled, *"Upon the death of M.* King *drowned in the Irish Seas,"* and a second poem, *"Elegy on Edward King,"* is, according to the standard edition by Morris and Withington, probably also by Cleveland. Elegiac verse was certainly one of the necessary exercises of the Cambridge undergraduate in these years.

Cleveland's life at Cambridge was a good one. He was well liked personally and well respected as a scholar. As one of his most devoted students and future editors wrote of him in later years, "Being thus well descended from a vein of Learning he even lisped wit, like an English *Bard*, and was early ripe for the University, who was one."[4] However, very little is known about the details of his undergraduate life at Cambridge. Apparently, he liked his tutor well enough to stay with him—as Milton notably did not. And, like Milton, he served late in his career as "Father" of the summer revels which had been traditional, with some interruptions and some opposition on the part of the older Fellows of the College, for many years at Christ's. Such a choice indicates several things: that Cleveland was popular with the undergraduates and Fellows and that Cleveland's wit was at that time highly enough regarded to entrust him with the position of master of ceremonies at a ceremony noted for its good-humored wit and its satirical treatment of members of the college community. It was important for the master of ceremonies to be witty and funny—something Milton had understood would be difficult for him, though the wit of his poem, "At a Vacation Exercise," is quite vital still. Berdan compliments Cleveland for having been funny and refreshing (while condemning Milton for being "too ponderous"), and he comments on the cleverness of Cleveland's effort and in particular on the cleverness of his puns. The orations presented on these occasions were usually filled with submerged puns—on names of students or Fellows and on university occasions—and Cleveland's punning on his being "Father" to his seniors (several undergraduates would also have been chosen to act as "sons" for the ceremony) was probably quite conventional.

Even before Cleveland had acted as master of ceremonies of the summer vacation exercises (many, if not most, students remained in college during vacations), he had been distinguished as an orator by being asked to give the Latin address of welcome in September,

1629, to the Chancellor of the university, the Earl of Holland and the successor to Buckingham. As Berdan and others note, among the dignitaries present was the French ambassador, and with him the great painter Peter Paul Rubens, who, like Van Dyck, had been courted by the king to remain in England. Cleveland was, of course, among the youngest students at the college at the time; and it is thought, as David Masson in his *Life of Milton* suggests, that the welcoming address was normally given by one of the younger, possibly one of the brighter, students.

John took his degree in 1631 and probably remained as a student at Christ's for the next three years, but there is no way of being certain that he did. He was elected to the Hebblethwaite Fellowship in Thomas Cleveland's college, St. John's (a larger college than Christ's) in 1634 and took his M.A. in 1635. Ordinarily, as a Fellow of St. John's, Cleveland would have proceeded to take religious orders within a six-year period; but Cleveland had been admitted, in 1640, to the Law Line instead. His study of the law helps explain how, at the end of his days, he was able to find refuge in Gray's Inn, where he eventually died. It is likely, though not certain, since the records are silent on this issue, that Cleveland also took a master's degree at Oxford: a normal procedure for that time. The date Anthony á Wood gives for a degree at Oxford is 1637; and, master's degree or not, Wood included Cleveland's biography in *Fasti Oxonienses*.

Apart from the standard responsibilities of teaching and studying, Cleveland undertook some unusual tasks during these years. He became Rhetoric Reader between 1635 and 1637 and had opportunities to address members of the college on several occasions. One of the most important addresses he gave, if not the most important, was in March, 1642, when he addressed the king himself *in extempore*. As Cleveland's editors of 1677 said, "The King called for him, and (with great expressions of kindness) gave him his hand to kiss, and commanded a Copy to be sent after him to *Huntington*, whither he was hastening that Night."[5] If the king thought highly of John Cleveland, John Cleveland thought most highly of him; he devoted much of the rest of his life to fighting the king's enemies.

II   *A Soldier for the King*

The last definite date which we can assign to Cleveland's days at Cambridge is June, 1642.[6] After that he removed himself to Oxford, the king's own camp, and then to the fortifications at Newark. These were, quite understandably, very difficult times for everyone in England. The Civil War itself had broken out in open hostilities in 1642, though troubles had been smoldering—as they always do—for many years before. From 1639, when Archibishop William Laud tried to impose Episcopalianism on the Presbyterian Scots, King Charles I and his government—a government without a Parliament, which ultimately held the purse strings—were in trouble. The two Bishops' Wars brought Charles's government to financial ruins and gave, unwittingly, the real power of government to Parliament. Though the first Bishops' War ended in a brief truce in 1639 at Berwick, the war was not over.

After Charles summoned his military adviser, the Earl of Strafford, from Ireland, the king called a Parliament to ask for almost a million pounds to fight the Scots. The "Short Parliament" was dissolved by the king only three weeks after it had met, since it was quite plain that it would not vote the money without important concessions being made. Ultimately, the Scottish army, under Alexander Leslie, moved across the border and occupied the North of England: the counties of Northumberland and Durham. The king's army, unable to fight, melted away; and Charles found himself paying the wages of what was left of his own forces, as well as the forces of the invader, until a new Parliament could be called. The "Long Parliament" was thus called, and the king's fate was virtually sealed: his ministers were either executed or exiled, including Strafford, his military arm (d. 1641), and Archbishop Laud, his religious advisor (d. 1645). Ultimately, the king took to the field against Parliament in August, 1642, after having sent Queen Henrietta Maria abroad to her native France in order to secure him whatever aid she could.

Cleveland himself left Cambridge for the king's headquarters in Oxford some time in either 1642 or 1643. The chances are that, while in Oxford, he wrote the piece which brought him into the pamphlet wars, "Character of a London Diurnal" (1644); and S.V. Gapp suggests that Cleveland may have gone to London to supervise a later edition of the work in 1645. Gapp's suggestion is based upon remarks dropped in *Mercurius Britannicus*, one of many papers being issued in London, though the paper may itself have been speculating on his whereabouts. It is certain, however, that Cleveland served with the garrison at Newark in Nottinghamshire as Judge Advocate.

Cleveland seems also to have been the principal with whom the

Scottish commander, David Leslie, treated while negotiating the surrender of the garrison in 1646. Leslie demanded the surrender on March 31, but Cleveland's replies indicated no intention of complying. Eventually, Cleveland turned the garrison over to the Scots on May 6 or 7, only a day or two after the king himself had surrendered. As Cleveland's editors observe, Cleveland was ready to sacrifice his life to his "Loyalty, had not the King's Especial Command, when first he had surrendered himself into the hands of the *Scots*, made such stubborn Loyalty a Crime."[7] There is a story that Leslie put Cleveland on trial after the surrender and then dramatically dismissed him as beneath his contempt; but, since it is known that Leslie left the garrison in great speed after the surrender, the likelihood is that no such trial took place.

III *Years of Wandering and Arrest*

The years immediately after the surrender of Newark are a problem for biographers. According to Berdan, one of the weekly papers for the opposition said as late as May 27, 1645, "Of our friend Cleveland, that grand malignant of Cambridge, we heare that he is now at Newarke."[8] But the chances are that he stayed at Newark not much longer, if at all, than Leslie did; the paper had merely not received information of the surrender by the time the article was composed. Berdan says, "For the next nine years and a half nothing is known of his life"[9]; and, unless some really conclusive evidence comes forward, the problem of what became of these years will persist. S. V. Gapp is the one scholar who feels he has solved at least some of the problem, and John Kimmey has accepted (Morris and Withington are more cautious) his views. Gapp contends that Cleveland spent the years until his eventual arrest at Norwich in 1655 as a writer for a number of underground papers in London, and the most notable among them was the *Mercurius Pragmaticus*, which Gapp suggests may have been totally the work of his hand at various times.

Of course, Gapp may be correct. It is certainly reasonable to think that the author of one of the most famous characters—and one which was enthusiastically imitated on all sides—as well as a number of the best verse satires written during the war—"The Rebell Scot" the most notable of them—would have gravitated toward the underground press and the sudden "mercuries" which were their expression. However, Gapp's position is based on conjecture, despite his care and great attention to detail. Among other things, he depends on a close reading of poems which are not in the received canon and of "mercuries" which, while probably referring to Cleveland, do not pinpoint his whereabouts.

One thing that does seem reasonable and certain is that Cleveland was in London for a while before 1655; but I emphasize, of course, that Gapp's views are not unreasonable, merely uncertain. Whatever Cleveland was doing—practicing law, in retirement, or involved in underground Royalist schemes—he is on record as having confessed to the authorities at Norwich that he came to that city "about a year since" from London. The fact that the authorities were even skeptical about Cleveland's business in Norwich is perhaps important; it either supports Gapp's association of Cleveland with the "mercuries" or invites suspicion of more dangerous connection. Berdan quotes from Thurloe's state papers the following letter, which I reproduce in its entirety:

May it please your lordship,
In observance to the orders of his highness and council sent unto us, we have this day sent to the garrison of Yarmouth one John Cleveland of Norwich, late judge advocate at Newark, who we have deemed to be comprized within the second head.

The reasons of judgment are;

1. He confesseth, that about a year since he came from London to the city of Norwich; and giveth no account of any business he hath there, only he pretends that Edward Cooke, Esq; maketh use of him to help him in his studies.

2. Mr. Cleveland confesseth, that he hath lived in the said mr. Cooke's house ever since he came to the said city, and never but once into the country. Indeed his privacy hath been such, that none or but a few save papists and cavaleeres did know, that there was any such person resident in these parts.

3. For that the place of the said mr. Cleveland his abode, viz. the said mr. Cooke's is a family of notorious disorder and where papists, delinquents, and other disaffected persons of the late king's party do often resort more than to any family in the said sity [sic] or county of Norfolk, as is commonly reported.

4. Mr. Cleveland liveth in a genteel garbe; yet he confesseth, that he hath no estate but 20£ per annum allowed by two gentlemen, and 30£ per annum by the said mr. Cooke.

5. Mr. Cleveland is a person of great abilities, and so able to do the greater disservice; all which we humbly submit, and remain,
Your honour's truly humble servants,
[fourteen signatures follow]
Norwich, Novemb. 10, 1655.[10]

YEARY LIBRARY
LAREDO JR. COLLEGE
LAREDO, TEXAS

What this letter ultimately means is that Cleveland was a suspicious character in a place and at a time when people with no visible means of support could be indicted for being informers or spies by what Berdan calls the local "village Dogberries." As a result of this letter, Cleveland spent at least three months in Yarmouth prison and ended, finally, by writing an appeal directly to Oliver Cromwell, Lord Protector. That such arrests were made from time to time for good reason is a matter of record; that just as many, or perhaps more, were made for no reason at all is also a matter of record. David Underdown, in his study of Royalist conspiracies in England during the period, emphasizes the fact that by 1655 most of the men (excepting, as he says, the hard core of prisoners) who supported the king in a military way were at liberty. And during this time there were innumerable rumors and scares, particularly in the North, where evidence of Royalist conspiracy had been plentiful only recently. The year 1655 saw a new military phase of Parliamentary government—in the form of a government by major generals. Of these major generals, Underdown points out that:

Under the "Orders for securing the peace of the Commonwealth," their supervision now became the new officials' principal duty. By this document the Cavaliers were divided into three categories: those guilty of subversive activity since the establishment of the Protectorate; those against whom recent sedition could not be proved, but who still showed themselves "by their words or actions" to be convinced Royalists, who were to be imprisoned or banished, retaining their estates; and those who had merely been guilty of delinquency in the civil wars, who were to be assessed for the Decimation Tax.[11]

Thus we see that the letter outlining reasons of judgment was operating under the second of the three categories ("comprized within the second head" as the letter states): "against whom recent sedition could not be proved" but who, "by words or actions," seemed still to be Royalist in sympathy.

Apparently not a great many arrests were made under this order, and those that were made ordinarily brought with them imprisonment for not much more than a year. Underdown actually cites Cleveland's arrest as an example of one of the notable figures who suffered. As a key to Cleveland's activities, we might consider the following statement of Underdown's: "Like the multitude of vagrants and 'idle persons' who found their way to prison under the

YEARY LIBRARY
LAREDO JR. COLLEGE
LAREDO, TEXAS

Major Generals' police powers, conspiratorial intentions need not always be ascribed to the victims."[12]

The letter Cleveland wrote, "To the Protector after long and vile Durance in Prison," is included in its entirety by Berdan, who considers it the best example of the poet's prose. It is indeed a moving document; and it, were we to take it at its word, could indicate that Cleveland had somehow made his peace with Parliament and the Commonwealth. The tone of the entire letter is marked by the mode of address to the protector, a mode formerly used for addressing kings and patrons, and one for which Cleveland's training must have been nearly perfect. The mode is characterized rather well by its opening statements, among them: "I address to your Highness, knowing no place in the nation is so remote as not to share in the ubiquity of your care, no prison so close as to shut me from partaking of your influence." But, more important than the tone or the form of the letter, which we consider later, is the fact that it contains a few scraps of information about the ten years' obscurity which ache so sharply for illumination. Cleveland tells us: "My Lord, it is my misfortune that, after ten years of retirement from being engaged in the differences of the State, having wound up myself in a private recess, and my comportment to the public being so inoffensive that in all this time neither fears nor jealousies have scrupled at my actions . . . ."[13]

He then suggests that there are but two reasons why he is imprisoned: his adherence to the Royalist cause (subtly put to possibly include a continuing loyalty as well as a past loyalty) and his poverty, asserting, as he does, that he is without ten acres to his name and thus unable to bail his way out. As he says, anyone with an estate is sure to be acquitted, while his own poverty keeps him prisoner. Cleveland, at any rate, maintains his profession of loyalty to his party as a virtue and not as a cause for imprisonment. He insists that he has been in retirement from active participation in the affairs of state, and, if true, this statement may be a disclaimer of even subversive journalistic activities of the sort Gapp assures us occupied his time until his arrest. Still, Cleveland's language is carefully enough couched that he could maintain his honesty while not admitting to any untoward actions.

At any rate, Cromwell responded by permitting his release; and if Berdan is correct in his guess, Cleveland was a free man in the summer of 1656. Where he went after his release is difficult to say,

but some reason exists for suspecting that he was in London, probably in Gray's Inn (possibly even practicing law) by the fall of 1657.
John Aubrey indicates in his biography that Cleveland and Samuel
Butler saw each other frequently in Gray's Inn during this last year
of Cleveland's life, and this assertion has contributed greatly to the
general view that Butler and Cleveland shared not only a similar
satirical bent but many hours of each other's company and were
good friends. As Aubrey says, "He [Cleveland], and Sam. Butler,
&c. of Grayes Inne, had a clubb every night. He was a comely
plump man, good curled haire, darke browne. Dyed of the scur-
vy . . . . "[14] The reference to Cleveland's portliness is by no means
a singular one, for the funeral elegy, written prematurely by
"S. H.," describes Cleveland as one "Whose face and belly were as
big as *Bens*"—a reference, of course, to the notable figure Ben
Jonson cut as a poet, doubtless, as well as a man.

IV *Death and Posthumous Publication*

Cleveland died only shortly after his return to London of what is
described as an intermittent fever. Aubrey apparently erred not
only about what eventually killed Cleveland but also about the place
of his burial. It may be superfluous to add that he also did not know
the date of Cleveland's death and wrote himself a note to question
Mr. Nayler about it. Berdan has Cleveland, at forty-five years of
age, dead on Thursday morning, April 29, 1658, and buried in St.
Michael Royal, the parish church, on College-Hill, London. He did
not live to see the collapse of the Commonwealth after Oliver
Cromwell's death and the succession (kinglike) of his son, Richard.
Only two years after Cleveland's death, the Crown was restored and
the Royalist party vindicated.

One of the most troublesome aspects of Cleveland's life is the fact
that he paid little or no attention to the publication of his work.
There is no certainty that he supervised the printing of his prose
satires, such as the character of the "London Diurnal," a work
which, if first written and printed in Oxford as assumed, he could
easily have seen through the press. Eleanor Withington assumes
that the poems were printed wholly without Cleveland's supervision or consent: a comment that can be made of much of the work of
seventeenth-century poets.

The first collected edition of his work was produced in 1647: one
prose character and seventeen poems, many of them added in sub-

sequent printings that year certainly by other hands. And, in fact, the problem that beset his modern editors was one early faced by those collecting his works. Once Cleveland's authorship was publicly noticed (first in 1651), numerous uncertain poems swelled the canon, virtually beyond the point of restoring order to it. Even today, after the remarkable and invaluable work of Morris and Withington, some thirteen poems can be described as only "probably" his. One of the motivations of Samuel Drake and John Lake's 1677 edition, which Berdan felt was the most reliable edition, was their concern for purging the spurious poems from the canon. Theirs was an early effort, however faulty, to devise the received canon.

Even Berdan and Morris and Withington have their disagreements, which show ultimately how difficult establishing the texts is. Berdan includes eighteen nonpolitical poems (from the 1677 edition), eleven political poems (also from the 1677 edition), and a total of eleven more poems which do not appear in the most reliable previous edition. Thus, the canon established by Berdan includes forty poems; but Morris and Withington include thirty genuine poems and thirteen "probable" poems. Of the poems Berdan accepts from the 1677 edition, Morris and Withington accept all but "The General Eclipse," which they relegate to the "Probable" status; they add two poems which they certainly accept: "Parting with a Freind upon the Rode," and the Latin, "Epitaphium Thomae Spell." In their section of poems probably by Cleveland, Morris and Withington accept only three of the poems Berdan accepted in his eleven poems additional to those appearing in the 1677 edition. Morris and Withington thus add nine poems to their "probable" list and eleven poems to the total canon, while striking eight of Berdan's poems, among which are three poems in tribute to Ben Jonson.

As we can see, the uncertainties which characterized John Cleveland's own times have repercussions in our own, and particularly in reference to working out and establishing the authorship of the very poems which made him famous. So many were anxious to puff his reputation and to benefit from it that they—often unwittingly—did him something of a disservice. We must also realize that it is the very nature of the uncertainties of his time which launched him into the adventures of literature to begin with. And it is unlikely that we would take much notice of him at all if he had not been compelled to write by the commitments he himself had made to his party. Out of these commitments have come his works. His wit, of course, was

natural and always there—as his university experience and reputation demonstrate. But Cleveland would quite likely not have become a public wit and a celebrated national wit had he not chosen to
defend the king with his pen as well as his "sword." His best work
was occasional, and we shall have opportunity in our critical discussions to examine the implications of this fact.

CHAPTER 2

"Clevelandism"

THOUGH the term never seems to have caught on or to have developed a wide currency, "Clevelandism" was a coinage which served Dryden in his attempt to define and condemn the peculiar use of language which marks Cleveland's more distinctive verse. Lisideus, Dryden's Francophile spokesman in *Of Dramatick Poesie*, describes another poet by referring to his tendency to "pay us with clenches upon words and a certain clownish kind of raillery" and to offer now and then "a Catacresis or Clevelandism, wresting and torturing a word into another meaning."[1] Thus Dryden sees Cleveland's style as depending upon a "wresting and torturing" of words out of their proper meaning as well as the wresting and torturing tropes—or figures of speech—out of their ordinary uses. Such a description tells us plainly that Dryden, the giant of the next generation of poets, thought Cleveland's style to be inappropriate and a disfigurement of the rules.

The preeminent critic who succeeded Dryden, Samuel Johnson, also had a distinct aversion to the "clench" or pun, which he sometimes referred to as "quibbles." And he had just as strong an aversion to torturing tropes or disfiguring language. He accuses poets like Cleveland of having a tendency to "enormous and disgusting hyperboles."[2] And, of course, both Johnson and Dryden—as well as a number of other passing commentators—accuse Cleveland of extremism in his use of language and tropes. The accusation has not only stuck fast, but the natural concomitant of such a judgment, that Cleveland is a decadent poet, has stuck along with it. Consequently, the present age accepts Cleveland as a curiosity, as an example of a practitioner in a good tradition—the Metaphysical—gone bad.

There is no reason why one must absolutely accept the views of the molders of neoclassical taste. For instance, while many critics might accept the fact that poetry such as Cleveland's should be decorous and that it fails when it is not, they may not accept Dry-den's view of what is decorous or successful. They may take issue, for example, with such evaluations as this of the most famous two lines of "The Rebel Scot":

> Had Cain been Scot God would have chang'd his doom;
> Not forc'd him wander, but confin'd him home,

Si sic, omnia dixisset! This is wit in all languages: 'tis like Mercury, never to be lost or kill'd.[3]

Whether this is wit in all languages or not is surely debatable: any age which does not hold that being a Scot is in and of itself humor-ous may take issue with Dryden's judgment. The point is, however, not whether or not Cleveland is witty—as indeed he is—but whether or not his wit is a decadent wit. We will see ultimately that it is often an indecorous wit; that it is a wit of extreme situations, that it creates those situations out of "ordinary" material; and that it is a wit which seems somewhat self-conscious. It may well be that this is the definition of decadent wit; but, if it is, so it may also be that it is not impossible to delight in such decadence.

I *Wit and Its Norms*

Cleveland's two poems on the subject of an hermaphrodite are excellent examples of what might be considered the norm of his wit. They are self-conscious efforts to push an idea to its very limits and to amuse, as they do so, a reader who might himself be trying to second-guess the poet. These poems offer a reasonable starting point because they do not contain famous lines which have appeared in critical estimates as examples of decadence. The first, "Upon an Hermophrodite," in a matter of sixty-six spritely lines explores the question of duality in the sex of the hermaphrodite, then duality in all of nature; touches on Adam and Eve, Venus and Adonis; and ends on an amusing note with Philip and Mary, who appear on a contemporary coin. It begins with a comic address:

> Sir, or Madame, chuse you whether,
> Nature twists you both together;
> And makes thy soule two garbes confess,
> Both peticoat and breeches-dress.

These four-beat couplets, reminiscent of the later *Hudibras* by Samuel Butler and somewhat of a prosodic break with the Metaphysical past, are quite suitable for the kind of surprise and "ringing home" which the two-line units of wit demand. In this sense, these lines are a greater link with the future than with the past; and they are particularly a link with the future of doggerel wit. But there is is something particularly intellectual about Cleveland's imagination. He is not content with amusing us by a comic situation or allusion, as Butler frequently is; he offers us a bit of subtlety. Before he begins his witty anatomy lesson in which all the parts of the body are seen to have their masculine and feminine analogues, and immediately after he offers the mixed address of "Sir, or Madame," Cleveland gives us this example of unexpected masculine-feminine conjunctions:

> Thus we chastise the God of *Wine*
> With water that is Feminine,
> Untill the cooler Nymph abate
> His wrath, and so concorporate.
>
> (5–8)

The wit is first in the allusion to the Latin: *Bacchus*, god of wine is masculine, while *aqua* is feminine, and then in the more abstruse word, "concorporate," meaning not only to meld together (thus going somewhat beyond conjunction) but suggesting also an assimilation so thorough it resembles the act of digestion, a particularly nice touch considering his subject. Perhaps wit in such a word is a Clevelandism; but, if it is not, it is still characteristic of Cleveland to depend on the effectiveness of a single, technical, and usually polysyllabic word to drive the final point home.

After this exordium, Cleveland cites Adam, in whom both sexes were "ingrost," and the fact that, even after Eve is created (with a clench), man and woman are still one in marriage:

> When providence our Sire did cleave,
> And out of *Adam* carved *Eve*,
> Then did man 'bout Wedlock treat
> To make his body up compleat.
>
> (11–14)

The clench is in the word "cleave" which means both join and sever, and the allusion to body sets up much of the rest of the poem: the anatomy lesson which looks for "a paire" in those things like lips, which can, by parting, "dispaire." For the purposes of the poem, any pair is a masculine and a feminine pair: the arms, the legs, the eyes ("Here *Venus*, there *Adonis* lyes") all are male and female. Even in "every single sound/A perfect Dialogue is found," and the breasts distinguish one another as sister and brother: a distinction which we might feel is a bit farfetched, though its position in the poem suggests not that it is a climactic trope, merely that it is one more in a succession of tropes. The succession of anatomical references is interrupted by a reference to Achilles in his disguise as Pyrrha at King Lycomedes' court (though Cleveland gives him the common name of Phillis, possibly for the sake of rhyming it with Achilles—itself something of a stroke of wit). After the right leg takes the left to dance and after it is finally admitted that the one part of the body which admits no change of gender is the heart, Cleveland concludes briefly, "Thus did natures mintage vary,/ / Coyning thee a *Philip and Mary*."

What characterizes the poem throughout is a relentless urge to search out the witty invention. The interruption of the reference to Achilles and Ulysses is typical and does not stand alone in the poem. Unity is not what Cleveland is after, though he enjoys the anatomical metaphor as long as it lasts—and it lasts throughout the core of the poem. But the poem neither begins nor ends with its controlling metaphor. It ends on an uncertain note: first a reference to Tib and Tom, possibly a phrase something like Jack and Jill, or perhaps a reference to a card game called Gleek (though Gleek has not two but three players, thus weakening the witty situation), then a reference to a coin on which Philip and Mary appear nearly interwined.

But there is no reason to suspect that Cleveland was unable to unify the poem. The wanton interruption of the catalog of anatomical tropes, an interruption which could perfectly easily have been delayed, suggests that Cleveland was intent upon avoiding the smooth unity that Dr. Johnson or we might have desired. There is a roughness to the verse, to be sure, and it may just be what Cleveland was aiming for—that he felt such rough wit needed rough verse, as he says in his poem on Guy Fawkes. The possibility that Cleveland was concerned with such a hypothetical decorum of wit is not particularly attractive; more attractive is the hypothesis that Cleveland had as a primary purpose the achievement not of unity or decorum but of some amusing and witty invention. The fact seems to be that Cleveland is willing to sacrifice a great deal to achieve his ends. For Johnson, he sacrificed too much. For his own time, however, he seems to have known just how much he could ignore and still delight his reader.

On the other hand, Cleveland's second poem on the subject of the hermaphrodite is rather different from his first. The first poem, with its roughness and humor, was included without Cleveland's permission in the 1640 edition of Thomas Randolph's poems as one of his own. Cleveland's second poem of sixty-two lines is really on the subject of his lost poem and the problems of paternity associated with poems which "stray." The poem treats in witty fashion sex, duality, and illegitimacy in highly allusive language. The five-foot line may signal a change in technique, though the use of the tight couplet is really not much different from its use in the first poem. What is different is that the controlling metaphors in the poem—not anatomy this time—seem to be maintained carefully throughout. The first metaphor is that of paternity: "Probleme of Sexes; must thou likewise bee / As disputable in thy Pedigree?" (1–2) and it not only opens the poem, but closes it: "Wee'l part the child, and yet commit no slaughter, / So shall it be thy Son, and yet my Daughter."

The second metaphor is an ecclesiastical pun on the then prevailing practice of a "Plurality of livings": "Never did steeple carry double truer, / His is the Donative, and mine the Cure." And though this metaphor is by no means scrupulously developed through the remainder of the sixty-two-line poem, it reappears in the reference to the apocryphal story of the female pope (along with the traditional name given to the pope's bastards: "nephew"):

> For you my brat that pose the porph'ry Chaire,
> Pope Iohn or Ioane, or whatsoe're you are,
> You are a Nephew. Grieve not at your state,
> For all the world is illegitimate.
>
> (51–54)

But, even with such relative unity, the poem is by no means a sharp break with its predecessor. It too strives for humor at almost any cost, willingly interrupting itself in order to invent wit. Cleveland virtually drops everything to work out an amusing sequence in which Parnassus itself becomes a cuckold hill on account of his poem's straying into Randolph's nest:

> Talke not of hornes, hornes are the Poets crest:
> For since the Muses left their former nest,
> To found a Nunnerie in *Randolphs* quill,
> Cuckold *Parnassus* is a forked hill.
>
> (29–32)

And this willingness to invent wit and to work the invention out even at the cost of developing material already in progress is characteristic of Cleveland's poetry.

We see it, along with a number of other developments, in such a poem as *"Upon a Miser that made a great Feast, and the next day dyed for griefe."* Among the developments is the beginnings of mastery of the five-foot line for witty purposes. For example, much of the humor of the poem is delivered in one-and-a-half line "clinchers" in this pattern: "is all this meat / Cook'd by a Limner for to view, not eat?" Though we must see, too, that Cleveland does not abandon the older and timeworn pattern of two full lines depending on their rhyme for the total impact of humor, such as: "Thus is the Feast a muster, not a fight; / Our weapons not for service, but for sight." The first pattern is most consistently used for purposes of witty amusement, particularly at the cost of the miser, whose food is being consumed as if by a hungry army. A military metaphor is picked up now and then for purposes of occasional wit, such as: "my weapon / Makes him an Eunuch, when it carves his Capon," which interrupt a mock-epic passage which itself has followed a passage which played on the notion of the feast's being movable, and thus perhaps religious in nature. And the poem ends with a typical clench (though these are not quite the final lines): "To vex him worse, / Death serves him up now as a second coorse." The pun is, as even a modern reader will agree, in rather an unpleasant strain. Imagining the miser as a corpse which is in turn a second course is doubtless the kind of "bad taste" which deeply offended Samuel Johnson. Cleveland delights in it, however, and puckishly follows with this clench and allusion to Thyestes' banquet: "Should we, like *Thracians*, our dead bodies eat, / He would have liv'd only to save his meat." It is a dashing, sometimes brilliant, poem of exceptional wit and intelligence.

Ultimately the poem is a character in the style of the incisive portraits of Samuel Butler's *Hudibras* and the perhaps more elegant, but nonetheless biting, portraits of John Dryden in his satires. It is impossible to say, of course, whether or not Cleveland had a specific miser and a specific feast in mind when he wrote this poem. And therefore it is all but impossible to make any generalizations about the relationship between this poem and the tradition of English satire that we associate with Butler and Dryden. If this poem is part of the tradition, the miser would be real and identifiable. However, Morris and Withington relate this poem to the satirical tradition of Lucian, Petronius, and Horace; thus indicating that their feeling is that the poem belongs to a larger, more impersonal form of satire than the English. Berdan is silent on this point altogether.

Perhaps another stock situation is being explored in "*A young Man to an Old Woman Courting him,*" in which Cleveland takes advantage of the opportunity to cast the character of an aging seductress. Cleveland delights in the opportunity and produces a carbuncular portrait. The poem begins with the expected—an immediate comparison with the arch-seductress, Eve:

> Peace Beldam *Eve:* surcease thy suit,
> There's no temptation in such fruit.
> No rotten Medlers, whil'st there be
> Whole Orchards in Virginitie.

The comparison is, to be sure, more waggish than merely conventional. It gives Cleveland the chance to unfold his final line, the hyperbole of orchards of virginity, and a line quite characteristic of him. In this four-foot line he uses the entirety of the couplet to complete his witty motion. We see, too, that in the first line, Cleveland experiments a bit with sound, and in "surcease thy suit" he permits the rapid sibilants to play on their own in an amusing way. It is not often that Cleveland achieves such an effect.

As in his other poems, Cleveland does not entirely abandon the imagery attached to Eve after the first few lines; it reappears sporadically thereafter, whenever it is useful for amusement. But the main thrust of the poem is at the "beldam's" age and the difficulties it represents for their engagement. A brief investment metaphor suggests that the young man's years would be mere interest when compared with hers; and another, more conventional, metaphor compares the connection with turning the year around: meeting January to December. Then, in a more surprising metaphor, Cleveland compares his lady with an Egyptian serpent who sheds its skin in order to return "unto his Prime."

This comparison gives him the chance to use an amusing couplet; "If my affection thou would'st win, / First cast thy Hieroglyphick skin." The use of the word, "Hieroglyphick," is particularly felicitous here, with its polysyllabic impact on otherwise ordinary lines. This, too, is an effect which Cleveland often strove for and often achieved. It is this very effect which Johnson resented in his complaints about the kind of language Cleveland preferred. Though we should see right away that the word is not a clench and not a trope. Its effectiveness is partly in its size, in its surprise, and in its aura of technical authority. It also suggests there is much to be read in those wrinkles. As A. Alvarez and others have indicated, Cleveland and Clevelandizers often sought for the word of extreme technicality (like Donne's "exantlations") to help develop the witty situation.

The poem ends with a sardonic promise that is reminiscent of some of Donne's lines in "Go and Catch a Falling Star": "When *AEtna's* fires shall undergo / The penance of the *Alpes* in snow," and many other impossibilities, Cleveland's young man says he will agree to take his "Madam Time," though, "I'le never be, 'stead of a Lover, / An aged Chronicles new Cover." Thus the entire poem is of the order of an exercise on a theme. The theme is the mismatch of old and young lovers, and the exercise is wholly one of wit: it is an effort to extract from the material every ounce of humor. The instruments which are applied to the situation are those of the clench, the learned reference, the allusion, the comic metaphor, and the subtle pressure of the rhymed couplet. Cleveland draws from his armory whatever instrument seems applicable at the moment; and he does it with no undue thought toward strict decorum or appropriateness, with no thought of remaining true to an extended metaphor for very long, and with no scruple at interrupting one developing image with a final and humorous couplet. Cleveland's aesthetic, in other words, is not predicated on the kind of unity we have since come to expect from a poem, a unity of structure and theme holds the poem together. But such a unity does not demand total obeisance: when the minor effect and humorous moment are in sight, Cleveland does not hesitate to abandon everything to capture it.

II   *Some Principles of Unity*

The fact that Cleveland wrote many poems with frequent breaks in their uniform texture does not mean that he was condemned to such a practice; he intended such breaks. In other words, he—and presumably much of his audience—felt it quite within his aesthetic rights to disregard unity for the purposes of isolated effect. He could use an alternative technique, as in his *"To Mrs. K. T. who askt him why hee was dumb,"* a poem which has a pleasant unity and whose purposes are not satirical or comic. Directly addressing "K. T.," the poet tells her in an easy-going manner that he might speak but Puritanism on the one hand and Catholicism on the other intervene to prevent his saying anything which might not give offense. Each stanza of this poem holds together in very easy fashion with no straining and with quite decorous imagery. Religious metaphors dominate the middle parts of the poem which are consonant with "your Religion which doth grant / A worship due to you my Saint"; and they suggest, as do the following lines, that Mrs. K. T. is a Catholic, one reason for his being dumb: "My ruder words would give offence / To such an hallow'd excellence; / As th'English Dialect would vary / The goodnesse of an *Ave Mary.*"

The poem ultimately shows itself to be playful and light; and it unifies the religious metaphor and the predicament of being dumb rather deftly in the final stanza:

> Oh listen with attentive sight
> To what my pratling eyes indite.
> Or (Lady) since 'tis in your choice,
> To give, or to suspend my voice,
> With the same key set ope the doore
> Wherewith you lockt it fast before;
> Kisse once againe, and when you thus
> Have doubly beene miraculous,
> My Muse shall write with Handmaid duty
> The Golden Legend of your Beauty.

The ease of tone and the uniformity of language give a completely different effect from that we have seen in other poems, but we can still see that Cleveland is writing a witty poem. The wit, however, does not seem to be its final objective.

A poem which achieves unity in a different way is his celebrated dialogue between a fair nymph and a black suitor in which unity is achieved most simply by the poem's being fashioned as a responsory. And, though there are moments in which the poem seems almost a question-answer structure, the principal source of unity is in the stichomythic [rapid-fire dialogue] repetition of a word or idea in subsequent speeches. When the nymph begins the poem by referring to a proverbial expression in which smoke is said to pursue the fair, the boy answers, "My face is smoak, thence be my guest / What flames within have scorch'd my brest." The nymph's reply plays upon the idea of flames, introduces the idea of the moon, which is in turn picked up in the boy's next speech, and so on through the poem. Cleveland respects this pattern throughout the entirety of this brief (thirty-line) poem; and, in the most important sense this pattern, in addition to its theme, is the poem's most distinguishing feature. One moment of not-quite typical Cleveland wit is in the image, one not particularly original, of the ink and press of the nymph's speech:

> Thy inke, my paper, make me guesse,
> Our Nuptiall bed will prove a Presse;
> And in our sports, if any come,
> They'l read a wanton Epigram.
>
> (19–22)

What characterizes this witty moment is the fact that it does not break the texture of the poem—it is not extreme in the sense that it reaches far from the immediate matter of the poem for the witty effect. All the materials are at hand: nothing has to be brushed aside in order to accommodate the figure. It is perhaps fair to say, however, that these lines are an example of wit, but not of a Clevelandism.

The kind of wit which delighted Cleveland's readers more than his treatment of black and white lovers is the type that characterizes "Mr. Cleuelands reply from Belvoir to the 3 Newarke Poets". In eighteen acidulous lines, Cleveland attacks three "Poetasters," who apparently thought they could outdo Cleveland in verse, by calling them dwarves and Tom Thumbs, but not before detailing the personal faults of each. Though the poem was never printed and appears only in Egerton Manuscript 2725, Berdan and Morris and Withington assume it to be genuine. The difficulties with the poem are not stylistic since, as Berdan says, the manner seems quite definitely Cleveland's. But the poem does use an unusual number of words which have not been satisfactorily tracked down, words which seem to have a Northern origin, but some of them may be connected with falconry. Morris and Withington discuss the problems presented by these words at length in their notes. The fact is, it may be argued, that the location of the garrison at Belvoir near Newark would place the three unknown poets (we do not know the occasion of their trespass against Cleveland) as possibly North-country men. Hence Cleveland's witty inventions may simply suit the situation.

The poem begins with a witty salutation: "All haile to the Poeticke Gleeke," which immediately establishes the poets' number as three, the persons of the game of Gleek. But there is, too, the obvious pun on "Greek," with the equally obvious, invidious comparison of the poetasters' work to the classics. He rails at them for being "The dwarfes, the Elues, Tom Thumbes in verse; / The very Jeoffryes of the times," Jeffery being the name of a well-known dwarf in Charles's court. Following his invention further, he presumes the dwarfs aspire to ale, being fit only for "buttermilke and whey," and that they also aspire to achieve the heights that Cleveland and the garrison at Belvoir possess. Thus the heights of Belvoir become a kind of Parnassus to which the "Poeticke Gleeke" incline. But Cleveland tells them plainly "Wee are high Comers, Birds of fame, / You are but Tonies of the game. / I will noe more Invention brew, / But cut the rope, and bid adieu." In this poem, as in others, Cleveland's invention is strictly for humorous purposes and, when it has run its course, the poem ends.

Cleveland's Belvoir poem (if indeed it is his) is not the only poem which treats poetic and rhetorical invention as if it were primarily an exercise in inventing likes. Poetic invention was, to be sure, vastly more complicated than simply finding similarities of a novel and instructive, not to mention humorous, order. But we must admit that the nature of witty invention was most exercised with finding things like (and, rarely, things unlike) his subject, by which the poet could illuminate it more grandly or more dramatically. Thus the simile and metaphor had long been the staple ingredient of poetry; thus, too, the conceit, a peculiar form of the metaphor, had become one of the principal ingredients of Metaphysical poetry. The Petrarchan mode had ultimately become a mode in which a range of metaphoric relationships became more or less standard—and stagnant—and lost thereby their original freshness. And Samuel Johnson, we may note, was concerned for the fantastical quality of Cleveland's invention when he accused him of creating outrageous hyperboles.

III *The Art of Invention: "Upon the death of M. King"*

Perhaps the single poem with the most disturbing and fantastic hyperboles and inventions is the elegy on Edward King. The fact that we have Milton's *Lycidas* in the same volume—*Justa Edwardo King* (1638)—is not likely to work in Cleveland's favor, though it must be admitted that the problems most critics have found with Cleveland's poem are not particularly connected with any comparative shortcomings. The shortcomings that critics see are those which have to do with Cleveland's pushing beyond the reasonable limits of wit. And, even though each age sets its own limits and each critic must satisfy himself *vis-a-vis* those limitations, Samuel Johnson is not the only major critic of Cleveland who condemns the poem. Even Morris and Withington suggest that the beginning of the poem is "an elaborate excuse for saying nothing, and the [imagery] suggests nothing beyond its own grotesque ingenuity" (lxxv). The poem begins:

> I like not tears in tune; nor will I prise
> His artificiall grief, that scannes his eyes:
> Mine weep down pious bead: but why should I
> Confine them to the Muses Rosarie?
> I am no Poet here; my penne's the spout
> Where the rain-water of my eyes runs out
> In pitie of that name, whose fate we see
> Thus copi'd out in griefs Hydrographie.
>
> (1–8)

What is most bothersome in this poem may not be the "grotesque ingenuity," a way of talking about the interest Cleveland (as an academic poet talking about a fellow academic) has in being inventive. Such invention would not necessarily be as decadent-sounding to the ears of those to whom the poem was addressed as it may be to ours. What is really most bothersome is the fact that Cleveland seems to contradict himself almost as soon as he has begun. He declares that he will not tolerate "tears in tune" or "artificiall grief," by which he naturally means metrical poetry about the poet's deep feelings and grief which is described according to the art (artificial) of invention. Any reader can see that Cleveland is, even while disclaiming being so, both tuneful and artificial.

It seems only reasonable to ask why. Cleveland knew as well as his readers that he was doing exactly what he disapproved.

Moreover it is reasonable to assume that he knew his audience was sensitive to the fact that he ignored his own caveat. Certainly no one could have missed the fact that his pen's becoming a tearful rain-spout is among the most frankly artificial expressions of grief in the language—if not *the* most artificial. Indeed, no explanation of this oddity has ever been satisfactorily given. It may be nothing more than, as Morris and Withington suggest, that these lines are an example of decadence and failure. Or we might presume that Cleveland is really condemning a practice, then illustrating that practice. The difficulty with such a reading is that there is no suggestion anywhere in the lines that Cleveland's claiming his "pious beads" of tears should not be confined to the "Muses Rosarie" is satirical. For Morris and Withington, the poem simply says that Cleveland abhors poets who can sit down and write tearful verse while actually feeling no serious emotions at all. For him, on the contrary, emotion bespeaks the poem. He writes about Edward King, his college mate and presumably his friend, not out of a sense of obligation to fill a memorial volume (a possibility he never mentions), but out of the intensity of his emotion—his grief.

The problem with this last interpretation, which is in most senses a reasonable one, is that the practice of the poem belies its purpose. Cleveland does not seem to express deep feelings of grief; and, judging by readers' responses, he has not elicited deep feelings of grief. That he strains to do both, however, is quite plain. The poem, in this sense, seems to be somewhat experimental. Instead of using normal means of expressing grief, Cleveland seems to substitute extremes of wit for extremes of feeling. It is as if he is relying on the peculiar intelligence of his academic audience—which knew him as Rhetoric Reader—to see that in the extremes of his invention are embedded the extremes of his grief. Such a reading is obviously speculative and by no means totally satisfying; its virtue is merely in its suggestion that there may be something which we do not, as later critics, appreciate in what Cleveland is doing. In other words, we avoid the absolute view that the poem is a failure.

There is, we must be prepared to admit, the possibility that Cleveland's audience would have expected no less from this master of wit, that they would have interpreted the extremes of his wit—since they had had some experience of it already—as an index to his feeling and to his effort on behalf of memorializing King. One curious detail which aids this reading is the fact that Milton's *Lycidas* is often attacked for reasons which are, basically, quite similar to those used in attacking Cleveland. *Lycidas* is often attacked for its having no genuine grief (by which is normally meant that it is not a romantic poem). But we know that *Lycidas* is not only one of the best poems of its kind (possibly the very best) but that it is also a poem in the most Miltonic manner that Milton was capable of at the time. Likewise, Cleveland's poem on King is, by all accounts, probably the most Clevelandized poem he ever wrote.

The evidence supplied to us by the other poems we have been discussing is strong in its insistence that Cleveland was not likely to have been naive in his expression in this memorial to King. The poem has most of the characteristics we have already seen: rhetorical inventiveness, a concern for developing the two-line unit as a compact witty instrument, and a reluctance to follow out or develop, as Morris and Withington put it, the image patterns or metaphors which yield their witty fruit only to wither instantly and not reappear. Also, we see, appropriately in this academic poem, a technique we have seen earlier, but which is here more fully developed: the introduction of learning and technical information into the poem.

Thus, as a way of reaching the two-line "clincher" he envisions, Cleveland recalls that recent and ancient speculation about the sea has yielded a conclusion:

> Some have affirm'd, that what on earth we find,
> The sea can parallel for shape and kind:
> Books, arts, and tongues were wanting; but in thee
> Neptune hath got an Universitie.
>
> (33–36)

The prevalence of the assumption that the sea had in it all analogues of things on earth is affirmed in Morris and Withington's footnotes. That King, because of his learning, was indeed a "universitie" is affirmed in King Charles's choosing him at an extremely early age, with only his bachelor's degree, for a tutor at Christ's College. It was a choice, to be sure, rammed down the throat of the college, but one which offended no one. We have no record of Milton's or anyone else's feeling that the choice was unwise. In fact, the most singular thing about King's appointment, and about the man himself, is that he was virtually universally loved.

We might also note in these lines that Cleveland's familiar device of "wrapping up" his unit of wit with a polysyllable, such as in "griefs Hydrographie," is quite effective here. Indeed, we observe that these lines are particularly felicitous in that regard: the word "Universitie" receives the same number of metrical accents as do "Books, arts, and tongues," with the pleasant addition, as is only proper, of an extra unaccented syllable.

The problem such a poem affords us is by no means a simple one. It may be that no age will ever again read it sympathetically. But it also seems true that for Cleveland grief and wit were by no means mutually exclusive, as they are for us and have been for some centuries. When we think of Milton's Hobson poems—exercises in the same vein as Cleveland's—we realize that what Cleveland did was not an isolated instance; and his success undoubtedly did not go unappreciated by his readers.

IV   *"The Hecatomb to His Mistresse"*

Though his readers doubtless appreciated poetical invention of the kind Cleveland was famous for, he was considerably conscious of what he was doing. Since he was quite conscious of his audience and of their expectations regarding his own performance, it is profitable for us to consider as a final poem in this chapter his hecatomb, or one-hundred-line "sacrificial offering," to his mistress. The poem is an elaborate mode of praising grandly all his mistress's "parts," but the principal issue of the poem is poetical invention; and its principal technique—apparently—is the renunciation of invention of similes and metaphors to "illustrate" the beauty of his mistress. He describes her in the final lines of "The Hecatomb to his Mistresse" as follows: "She that can strike the best invention dead, / Till bafled Poetry hangs down her head, / She, she it is that doth contain all bliss, / And makes the world but her Periphrasis" (97–100.) We observe with no small delight that, despite invention's having been struck dead, Cleveland immediately responds by celebrating its rebirth. In these lines alone he invents metaphor in abundance and personification in particular. But above all, perhaps, he "invents" the one hundredth line of his "hecatomb," a poem which could have little excuse for its length other than the justification of its symmetry as an offering.

Readers of English poetry are not surprised by a poet who announces renunciation of metaphor and elaborate language and does

so by means of metaphor and elaborate language, thus creating a
witty invention. But Cleveland's one hundred lines are a *tour de
force* for those of us who know what to expect. He begins with a
bombastic mock-address to the fraternity:

> Be dumb ye beggers of the rhiming trade,
> Geld your lose wits, and let your Muse be splaid.
> Charge not the parish with your bastard phrase
> Of Balm, Elixar, both the Indias,
> Of shrine, saint, sacriledge, and such as these
> Expressions, common as your Mistresses.

And in this address he gives his invention free rein to work at length
on the jaded nags of rhyme: urging them to geld themselves (being
masculine) and spay their muses (who are feminine). Typically, the
equine invention is useful for the moment, and then remorselessly
abandoned. As he explains in the following lines, "My text defeats
your art," which is to say his subject, his mistress, cannot be treated
by the art (of invention) of such "beggers" partly because they are,
indeed, beggars and have nothing of their own; but it is also because
his "text" is "Illustrated by nothing but her self" (10). Other poets
cannot understand this fact because, most importantly, their mistresses need the benefit of every artificial rhetorical and poetical
argument.

Because of their poverty, Cleveland spends some of the original
energy of the poem inventing on the subject of rhyming beggars
rather than on his mistress, though of course he does not abandon
her to an uninvented reverence. He compares the poets to spiders
who "travel by their bowels spun," what may be a rather indelicate
comparison; but, when it comes to his mistress, he pretends his
invention fails totally. He experiments with invention by contrast
rather than by comparison: "So can I not define how sweet, how
fair, / Onely I say she's not as others are" (35–36). But, all this while
he has also been toying with a metaphysical problem: the problem
attending to perception of pure substance, which is what he imagines his mistress to be. As he knows, such perception is impossible and thus all rules of invention, based since the time of Ramus
and before on sense, are irrelevant. Cleveland sounds almost like
Donne when, explaining the problem, he says, "As then a purer
substance is defin'd / But by an heap of Negatives combin'd"; and,
since Cleveland's mistress is a spirit, she has "no matter, no mor-

talitie" (34). Thus, as he says in the same passage, "For what perfec-
tions we to others grant, / It is her sole perfection to want"—or her
sole perfection is to be pure substance and to lack ("want") the
material qualities which are praised in others.

Naturally, such a "want" gives rise to considerable ingenuity of
invention. The very opportunity to treat abstract, almost medieval,
philosophical issues had long been the delight of learned poets,
particularly of the Metaphysical stripe; and Cleveland's approach is
by no means unfamiliar. In lines 45–50 he establishes the fact that
philosophy linked specific objects with specific senses while insisting that those objects which had multiple links with numerous
senses were "*common sensibles*." "So is't with her who, stinted unto
none, / Unites all Sences in each action." The lines which follow do
their best to unite the senses in their appreciation of his mistress
and they end with "Or can your sight be deaf to such a quick / And
well-tun'd face, such moving Rhetorick?" (57–58). Ultimately, as we
would expect, sense itself is "Corrupted with the objects excellence."

What follows is a mockery of the ordinary poets' approach to such
a problem. Lines 67–90 surrender the metaphysical argument about
sensory perception and attack the "man of mouth, that canst not
name a She / Unless all nature pay a subsidie." He encourages
rhymsters to find in their mistresses all impossibilities; and, as if
commenting on Fuller's life about himself, Cleveland invites the
poets to "come aloft, come, come and breath a vein, / And give some
vent unto thy daring strain" (75–76). As Fuller says, "Some distinguish between the *Veine* and *Strain* of Poetry, making the former to
flow with facility, the latter press'd with pains, and forced with
industry."[4] These Cleveland lines are doubtless more strain than
vein:

> Call her the Metaphysicks of her Sex,
> And say she tortures wits, as *Quartans* vex
> Physitians; call her the *Square Circle*, say
> She is the very rule of *Algebra*.
> What ere thou understand'st not, say't of her,
> For that's the way to write her Character.

> (81–86)

As a commentary on contemporary poetic invention, such lines
would have pleased even Samuel Johnson. But, as we realize, it is

itself a witty way of praising his lady: "She that affords poor mortals not a glance / Of knowledge, but is known by ignorance."

The witty hecatomb is instructive on several counts. Not only does it give us some insight (perhaps unnecessary, of course) into the practice of invention on the part of those poets Cleveland dislikes, but it also gives us an indication of the degree to which invention is consciously practiced by Cleveland himself. As moderns, we sometimes tend to think of analysis by invention as something which is *post facto*, an operation of the critic in his efforts to describe a poem; but Cleveland shows us unambiguously that such is not the case. Invention is, as its name implies, not a function of the critic but of the creator, of the poet.

Therefore, the term "Clevelandism," applied invidiously or not, is a term which finally aims at describing the kinds of invention Cleveland found of particular use. It aims, too, at emphasizing the characteristic ways in which wit functions in Cleveland's poems, just as it aims at describing the lengths Cleveland sometimes goes to achieve a witty situation. The term, in other words, is not necessarily limited to the abuse of a word or a phrase; it can be applied to the peculiarities of structure which identify many of the poems we have been discussing and which identify many we are yet to discuss. As study shows, some of the most notable "Clevelandisms" are not in the poems discussed in this chapter; however, the peculiarities of style, wit, and language found in these minor poems characterize the better-known lyrics and satires.

CHAPTER 3

Cleveland's Lyric Voice

I *The Mark Antony Songs*

IT is too bad that the music to which "A Song of Marke Anthony"
and "The Authours Mock-Song to Marke Anthony" were set is
lost to us. In these two remarkable and antithetical poems, Cleveland exercises the kind of ingenuity we expect of him; and it would
be natural for him to play not only against the ordinary concepts
associated with love-lyrics, in terms of image and association, but
also against the kinds of norms which would be established in the
minds of his listeners for the music to which such lyrics are set. The
meter of these poems, with their preponderance of three-beat mea-
sures, suggests a peculiarly rich musical background; and a knowledge of it would unquestionably contribute to our delight in hear-
ing them as songs.

What we first observe is that they are a brace of poems that are
not meant to stand individually, and they are not really impressive
by themselves. But together they are amusing and illuminating.
The situation of the first—and more "normal"—song is familiar.
Venus invites the poet-songster "Unto a fragrant field with Roses
crown'd" where she had previously prepared the scene with his
"wishes complement": his unspoken ideal woman, who is never
named and but little described. The images Cleveland uses for her
are singularly commonplace: "cherry cheekes" on which his eyes
"feasted"; "warmer lips" which he "tasted"; and a considerable
quantity of "golden hayre." All this imagery is conventional to the
point of being dull. Yet we find some of the intellectual developments with which we should be familiar.

For example, in dealing with a description of love in the final
stanza, Cleveland loads almost every possible relevant area of university study into his poetic muzzle and fires suddenly; and the
effect is humorous and astounding:

> Mysticall Grammer of amorous glances,
> Feeling of pulses, the Phisike of Love,
> Rhetoricall courtings, and Musicall Dances;
> Numbring of kisses Arithmeticke prove.
>   Eyes like Astronomy,
>   Streight limbs Geometry,
>   In her arts ingeny
>   Our wits were sharpe and keene,
>   Never Marke Anthony
>   Dallied more wantonly
>   With the faire Egyptian Queen.

The progress from grammar to arithmetic is in itself fantastic, but adding astronomy, geometry, and engineering into the bargain does nothing but make the already amusing situation broadly comic. In some ways this poem, like the hecatomb to his mistress, relies on a knowledge of what other songsters were saying and on the hope that his broad exaggeration will reveal them as incompetents.

Matched with this poem is the mock song whose purposes are not to poke fun at the competition but to reveal Cleveland's own "ingeny" in his ability to take the self-same situation and the self-same sweet lyric melody and turn them to the darkest of Plutonian purposes. The mock-song is an example of antilyric and perhaps even "black humor" of a sort that Robert Herrick and other seventeenth-century poets sometimes produced. Instead of having Venus draw him sweetly to his dreamed-of mistress in the evening protected by the sweet-singing nightingale, we have:

> When as the Night-raven sung Pluto's Mattins,
> And *Cerberus* cried three Amens at a houle;
> When night-wandring Witches put on their pattins,
> Midnight as darke as their faces are foule,
>   Then did the Furies doome
>   That my night-mare should come;

Thus the "faire Egyptian Queen" becomes a "foule Gipsie Queane" whose head is "Epicaene," whose cheeks are "gooseberry," and whose lips are "blewer."

But Cleveland's most ambitious invention is reserved for the last stanza, which is an analogue for the final stanza of the "Song." Instead of finding legitimate sciences figuring prominently in the last stanza, we find sciences of a thoroughly questionable sort, those which moderns still associate with Gypsies:

> Mysticall Magicke of conjuring wrinckles
> Feeling of pulses, the Palmestry of Haggs,
> Scolding out belches for Rhetoricke twinckles,
> With three teeth in her head like to three gaggs;
>   Rainbowes about her eyes,
>   And her nose weatherwise;
>   From them their Almanacke lies
>   Frost, Pond, and Rivers gleane.
>   Never did Incubus
>   Touch such a filthy Sus,
>   As was this foule Gipsie Queane.

This stanza is indeed brilliant, but its effectiveness would be paltry in comparison to what it is if it did not have the remarkable counterpoint of the complementary stanza in the "Song." In this sense, the word "counterpoint" is, perhaps, not so metaphorically restricted as it seems. The antiphonal value of the poems is not inconsiderable and may possibly be one of their most important qualities.

Beyond the obvious musical value of such antiphony there is another value which we should consider. The poems are complementary and antithetic, as we have observed, in a way which is not uncommon for the seventeenth century. We might go further in suggesting that there is a kind of argumentative counterplay in these poems, such as we find in poems like "L'Allegro" and "Il Penseroso" or in the myriad exercises Cambridge students performed on stated themes, like the Prolusions of Milton on such subjects as whether night is better than day. In Milton's Prolusions, we have only one side of an argument which plainly had two sides and two contestants. With Cleveland's two songs, we have both sides; and we see that both sides work with and against each other in mutual amplifications, as Milton's twin poems do. These poems present two sides of an argument: that a venereal adventure is divine and restorative or that it is serbonian and destructive. These ambivalences were commonly associated, as we know, with Mark Anthony and Cleopatra, though the poems are not "about" these figures.

What is important is that the poems are an exercise. They are self-conscious, cerebral, and carefully structured. Like so many of Cleveland's poems, they seem to be set pieces: tasks of a poetic order that the poet has set for himself. Such an observation would have been undisturbing to a seventeenth-century reader, who would have thought such a procedure to be quite natural; but for today's reader—and for any reader since, probably, the time of

Wordsworth and the romantics—such a fact is disqualifying. Instead of thinking of this poem as an exacting and amusing exercise, we are likely to think of it as a mere exercise; but, we should see that Cleveland is in remarkable control of his material in these two poems. Unlike some of the earlier poems we have discussed, these are not marked by the same kinds of witty expeditions which characterize, say, "Upon a Miser that made a great Feast." Rather, the witty amusement comes from the careful balance of images and statements, such as the opposition of "feare of surfetting" with "feare of vomiting" and "faire Egyptian Queen" with "foule Gipsie Queane." Thus, Cleveland's structural principles are clearly set and clearly followed. He was not a poet to be incapacitated by structural or symmetrical necessities.

One problem these poems present us is the textual one which appears in Morris and Withington's edition. The versions they print, which I rely on here, have five stanzas for the song and only four for the mock-song. Stanza three of the song is omitted in Berdan's edition, thus making both poems of four stanzas. This inconsistency is somewhat perplexing and points to the possibility that another stanza for the mock-song may have at one time been written, though it does not seem to have survived. The third stanza in Morris and Withington's edition begins, "Then in her golden Hayre I my armes twined"; and it seems to have its analogue in stanza three of the mock-song, which begins, "Like snakes engendring were platted her tresses."

Thus it is stanza four of the song, included in both modern editions, which seems to have no analogue in the mock-song. Its subject is the gazing into a mirror that turns out to be the eyes of the poet, which ultimately produces: "And by reflexive shine / I in her eye was seene." However, the problem is compounded by the fact that this fourth stanza has line analogues with the third of the mock-song. For instance, the first line of the fourth stanza of the song is "Wanting a glasse to pleat those amber tresses," which obviously parallels the line which mentions snakes and tresses. The existence of this line would seem to imply that the song has two stanzas which could parallel stanza three of the mock-song and that one of the stanzas was not meant to see print in a final version. Such reasoning is speculative, of course, and the likelihood is that we will never solve the problem unless a new stanza for the mock-song is discovered. Morris and Withington are deeply concerned with the textual problems of these poems, and their edition should be consulted for more information (see pp. xxxv and 132). Their concern is so deep that they admit fear that the song may not actually be Cleveland's, though both they and Berdan include the poem in the canon.

II *Sex, Love, War, and Metaphor*

"To the State of Love, or, *The Senses Festival*," is a poem which may be more recognizably in Cleveland's style, at least in so far as it has a couplet in its first stanza which George Williamson calls pure Cleveland: "Beauties chiefest Maid of Honour, / You may break Lent with looking on her." But, of course, there is much more to this poem than merely these striking lines; however, it should be pointed out as well that there is nothing else in the poem which is of quite the same quality. It begins with the sight of his mistress, his clasping her, then his kissing her, and finally his contemplating the fact that they are two souls reconnoitering each other—a thought appropriate to the dream-vision of the opening lines. The poem is six stanzas, and more than seventy-five lines, long. The stanza pattern suggests that this poem, too, might have been sung at one time. The poem has no controlling metaphor, as such, but does have a most curious controlling idea that is plainly expressed in the first lines of the poem:

> I saw a Vision yesternight
> Enough to sate a *Seekers* sight:
> I wisht my self a *Shaker* there,
> And her quick Pants my trembling sphear.

And the rest of the poem is a description of the dream-vision with particular emphasis on her radiance: "She so glittering bright / You'd think her soul an *Adamite*." This poem is the record of the senses' festival, to be sure; but the festival is a most platonic one, and the entire experience thus transformed into a religious ecstasy. The seventeenth century was no stranger to such *ecstasis*, as the readers of Donne and Herbert well know; and the purposes to which Cleveland puts such a vision are relatively familiar. Cleveland has, by virtue of his recording the vision, no limits to his imagination. Thus he imagines his mistress to be brown: "A brown for which Heaven would disband / The Gallaxye, and stars be tann'd." She is, we are told, "Sun-burnt with lustre of her own."

But there is nothing in Cleveland's poem of the deep (or high) purposes which Donne in "The Ecstasy" is capable of conceiving. Instead, Cleveland contents himself with using the metaphysical situation for its inherent witty possibilities. The religious images involve numerous religions, from Muhammadanism to Christianity, and offer considerable opportunity to invent wit, as in the statement that her kisses are so sweet "there is no tongue can phras't, / Till transubstantiate with a taste. / Inspir'd like *Mahomet* from above, / By th' billing of my heav'nly Dove." Or, "No Rosary this Votress needs, / Her very syllables are beads." But one of the most witty of the images Cleveland works into the poem is the continuing metaphor of warfare.

Part of the effect of this metaphor is secured by the fact that, while it is not inappropriate in connection with a description of would-be lovers, it is weirdly out of place in such a dream-vision. The mixture of warfare and religion is not novel, certainly, but mixing both together in the way Cleveland does gives a most uncanny air to the poem. In the fourth stanza, discussing the "jelly'd Philtre of her lips," the poet says, "Our Mouthes encountering at the sport, / My slippery soul had quit the fort, / But that she stopt the Salley-port." There is a marvelous dislocation in these lines which plays upon the corporeality of normal lovers and the dangers tradition associates with kissing ghostly beings. But that dislocation is of little consequence in comparison with the worldliness that invests the vision in the last stanza:

> Yet that's but a preludious bliss;
> Two souls pickearing in a kiss.
> Embraces do but draw the Line,
> 'Tis storming that must take her in.
> When Bodies joyn, and victory hovers
> 'Twixt the equal fluttering Lovers,
> This is the game.

Thus we see that in fact the entire poem is something "preludious." The contact of souls is a mere skirmish ("pickearing") to the formal drawing of lines of battle, when "Bodies joyn," and when, finally, "the pass is got" (76). Such military imagery suggests that this dream-vision is less religious *ecstasis* than wish-fulfillment.

A comparison of "The Senses Festival" with his much more successful and amusing "The Antiplatonick" might point to the possibility that both poems were part of the vogue which encouraged poems of platonic love and its antithesis. "The Senses Festival" is in its own odd way a poem about platonic love, though it breaks down, just as the vision seems to break down under the weight of the final metaphors. But the fact that "The Antiplatonick" is so much more successful than its possible counterpart, as well as the fact that the poem also ends with a volley of military images, could well point toward where Cleveland's sympathies, if not genius, lie. The poem has six stanzas totaling forty-eight lines and it disputes the value of love that merely resides in "Contemplation." Cleveland will have none of it; and his poem's military metaphors barrage the position of the platonist until it gives way. The fifth stanza of the poem shows quite clearly the power of the military metaphor, and the degree to which the poem is indeed antiplatonic:

> The souldier, that man of Iron,
> Whom Ribs of *Horror* all inviron,
> That's strung with Wire, in stead of Veins,
> In whose imbraces you're in chains,
> Let a Magnetick Girle appear,
> Straight he turns *Cupids* Cuiraseer.
> Love storms his lips, and takes the Fortresse in,
> For all the Brisled Turn-pikes of his chin.

Even military might is no match for the power of love, which as usual conquers all. And a close comparison of this stanza with the final stanza of "Senses Festival" shows that not only are many of the same terms used in both poems but the power of love is also seen to be equally strong and equally physical, though we must admit that the point of the fifth stanza of "The Antiplatonick" is to show that love is capable of overcoming even the force of arms. Thus what Cleveland may be doing in both poems could be quite clever: in the first, he takes the platonic situation and renders it more and more physical; in the second, he takes the physical and renders it more and more platonic. Yet he does not "break through" in either poem sufficiently enough to disturb his premises.

But the fifth stanza of "The Senses Festival" is not the one which would arrest the eye of the student of Cleveland. If anything, the first lines of the poem would indicate that Cleveland was in his usual "form": "For shame, thou everlasting Woer, / Still saying Grace and ne're fall to her!" These lines are not an example of catachresis, but an example of the kind of curious disjunction Cleveland specialized in: matching the ordinary imagery of a man sitting at a table before his meal saying Grace with the equally ordinary imagery of a wooer contemplating his mistress. The carnality of the situation is nowhere more heightened than in the yoking of these two commonplace images, and the effect is achieved almost effortlessly. There are a few nice touches also worth observing; for instance, the feminine rhyme is peculiarly striking because it receives a full accent and seems to be compressed into one syllable instead of two. And, though the version of the text I quote has two four-foot lines, another version, the one Berdan prints, has the second line as a five-foot line: "Still saying grace and never falling to her!" Nothing is really gained by normalizing the second line since the Berdan version is quite effective, but what is lost is something in the clarity of the line, though it may be, too, that the compression ultimately adds to the effect. In addition, there is the energy implicit in the power of the admonishment, and the same is true of the first line of Donne's "Canonization" and for the same reason: we rarely expect poems, particularly of this period, to begin with such a strong and ultimately disjunctive admonishment.

The rest of the poem is liberally sprinkled with witty couplets. After having referred to the "un-relenting She" as "a Dame of stone, / The Widow of Pigmalion," he explains that: "Love melts the rigor which the rocks have bred, / A flint will break upon a Feather-bed" (15–16). This celebration of the power of love parallels the celebration of love's power over the man-in-arms of the fifth stanza; it is an example of the way the platonic power of love can emerge from its other-worldness and conquer the flinty reality of this world. And love is not only capable of conquering arms and the stoniness of indifference, it can quell the power of reason as well. As Cleveland says:

> Vertue's no more in Woman-kind
> But the green-sicknesse of the mind.
> Philosophy, their new delight,
> A kind of Charcoal Appetite.
> There is no Sophistry prevails,
> Where all-convincing Love assails.
>   (25–30)

But the charming irony of the poem is that the poem itself has a "reasonable" cast to it; it presents an argument, or series of them;

then it resolves the argument with a conclusion in the best Cambridge academic tradition (preserving all the while the military metaphor):

> Since Loves Artillery then checks
> The Breast-works of the firmest Sex,
> Come let us in Affections Riot,
> Th' are sickly pleasures keep a Diet.

Thus the final goal of the antiplatonic analysis is riot "bold and free, / Not Eunuch't with Formality." Venus conquers all, and there is no ambiguity of souls "pickearing" round about each other; instead, we have the irresistible assault of "Loves Artillery."

The use of military metaphors in love lyrics is quite common for Cleveland. Perhaps it was due to his own military experiences or to the fact that the entire country had been deeply involved in the military struggles of the Civil War during the time when the poems were probably written; but, whatever the cause, Cleveland knew the terminology and the science of war well enough to use its situations in witty ways.

"To Julia to expedite Her Promise" encourages the lady by reason, analogy, and wit to hasten in making love to the poet, as she had promised. Each stanza has a core of metaphor or allusion holding it together, and the entire fifty-four lines are secured by their reference to the lady's delay. After having encouraged Julia to "Live double" because her "Sex lives faster than the males," he asks:

> How can thy Fortresse ever stand
>   If't be not man'd?
> The Siege so gaines upon the Place
> Thoul't find the Trenches in thy Face.
> Pitty thy self then, if not me,
> And hold not out, least (like *Ostend*) thou be
> Nothing but Rubbish at Deliverie.
>
> (21–27)

Though the image holds up well enough and even delivers its charge of wit in still surprising ways, we feel ultimately that the comparison of the final condition of Ostend and the projected final condition of the aged Julia if she fails to expedite her promise is basically flat. Unlike the images of the supping man saying Grace before his mistress, the surprise element is not followed up by the suggestion of a meaning which might have gone unsuspected except at second thought. Rather, we feel that the comparison with Ostend achieves little more than the felicity of working out the military metaphor already afoot. And this third stanza, of six, is actually the only stanza which fully depends on a military metaphor for its effect.

Other metaphors which energize the poem—though it is by no means one of the strongest of Cleveland's lyrics—fall into relatively conventional patterns. Since the poem is basically a *carpe diem* poem—with echoes of both Herrick and Donne, along with most other poets who tried the mode—time is a principal concern. As I have already indicated, Cleveland suggests that his Julia must move quickly since she is fated to live at a speedier rate than a man: "As if to measure Age's span / The Sober *Julian* were th' Account of Man, / Whil'st You live by the fleet *Gregorian*" (16–18). And, while the metaphor is again quite fitting, it stops right there. It is amusing even though, as Morris and Withington state in their notes, the fleet Gregorian calendar is all of ten minutes a year faster than the Julian; but, once amused, the reader must stop; he will not expect to be much enlightened. One of the unusual aspects of the metaphor—for Cleveland's work, that is—is the fact that there is little or nothing unsuspected about the comparison or its results. There is none of the unexpectedness that we prize in such "stretched" metaphors as we have seen earlier, and there is none of the synergism of those comparisons that we think of as more akin to Clevelandisms. The wit, as Dryden might say, is wit in all languages, but it is little more than that.

Wit may be enough, as we know; and it often is in many poems we value highly. The purposes to which the wit is directed are perfectly conventional: convincing Julia that she should not "flie / Incumbency" (itself a nice image) now. This poem is not one half of an argument for which there is a matching and antithetical poem, though such a practice was common enough, as we know from Sir Walter Raleigh's and Christopher Marlowe's poems on the subject; rather, it is a mock-serious, mock-careful effort on the part of the poet to use logic and rhetoric in the purposes of seduction. The seventeenth century is filled with such poems and with such a penchant for disputatiousness. The fact that Julia would never have been trained as a "school-divine" in the colleges of Cambridge puts her at a powerful disadvantage, as we can imagine. Consequently, the logician could be fanciful and fallacious without fearing that his

deception would be thrown back on him. The elements of wit
Cleveland uses in the poem are fanciful and by no means examples
of rigorous or thoroughgoing logical connections, but they have the
air of being rigorous and reasonable.

III *Love's Logic*

Much of the pleasure a seventeenth-century audience derived
from such poems was in seeing how the "logic" works. And, since it
is plain that only a male audience would have been able to appreciate the niceties of the logical wit-play, a poem such as "To Julia
to expedite Her Promise" is something of a curiosity. It seems to be
addressed to a woman and therefore has no real obligations to being
absolutely "logical" in anything but appearance.[1] But, since it is
read and appreciated by men who are trained logicians (as every
Cambridge man was), it must be close enough to being plausible to
elicit delight in the perception of just how far it falls short. Thus,
too, we see that the metaphors and the images are often those that
would not just occur to a man but would actually appeal to him. If
the poet were in earnest in addressing a woman, he would not insist
on the technicalities inherent in the military metaphors Cleveland
uses at length. Those technicalities were known to men, military
men, and would have "argued" most successfully with them.

We should consider, too, the appeal—logical and otherwise—
such images as the following, from stanza one of the poem, would
have for the woman who seems to be the object of the poetic address:

> Panting Expectance makes us prove
> The Anticks of benighted Love,
> And withered Mates when wedlock joynes,
> Th' are Hymens Monkeys which he ties by th' loynes,
> To play (alas!) but at Rebated Foynes.

"Rebated Foynes" are foils whose sharp points are covered and
dulled so that no genuine wounds could be garnered from a fight.
Thus "Panting Expectance" has a debasing quality to it by virtue of
its association with a false duel; its association with their false love
(because always in expectancy) which, in their waiting, makes them
"Anticks" or antiques; and its association with age and withering,
making them as debased as Hymen's monkeys, who, being tied at
the loins, become a joke in exceedingly bad taste.

There is no question but that the appeal such imagery would have had to Julia either would have been quite limited or would have alienated her entirely. Designed not to appeal to her in a convincing manner, it appeals in an amusing manner to the male audience for whom the poem seems primarily destined. But the poetry itself, the individual images, and their strategic placement—not to mention numerous other conscious devices in the poem—are organized in order to argue a case, which is the norm for most *carpe diem* poetry. In this sense, the poem is not unlike "To His Coy Mistress," which, with its learned allusions and careful balance, is a delight to those in on the joke, but it is not a poem whose reasoning is so airtight that its conclusions seem plausible.

In other words, and to deal with Cleveland's poem from a slightly different "angle," "To Julia" is, like much of his poetry, an exercise in a mode. The mode is the *carpe diem*, and the method is the normal logical-rhetorical one of argument and conclusion. And the fact that the poem is undistinguished is less a fault of its convention-ality than of the fact that Cleveland's invention is wanting. It may also be a fault that Cleveland's poem does not appeal to his intended female "audience," Julia, as well as it does to his male audience. No one could long assume that this is a poem intended for the purposes of seduction; it does not transcend its function as a pleas-ant exercise.

IV   *"Fuscara": Stretching the Norm*

"Fuscara; or The Bee Errant" gives less the impression of being a mere exercise than some of the poems which we could properly consider part of Cleveland's lyric mode. One of Cleveland's best-known poems, "Fuscara" is a lengthy excursion of eighty-two lines that is somewhat reminiscent of Donne's "The Flea," since Cleve-land's poem details the travels of a bee on the person of a brown lady, Fuscara, and, though full and ripe with some of Cleveland's best invention, it gives less of the feel of the disputation than the poems we have been discussing; and it may also be said that it is ultimately less peculiar to Cleveland's manner. Yet, this poem, apart from "Rebell Scot," is most frequently anthologized by modern editors. The reason is simple: the poem is a curious example of the extended conceit and is useful in illustrating the device as it de-veloped late in the tradition.

The basic conceit is of the bee, "Natures Confectioner," which explores the most beautiful of the flowers: Cleveland's darksome beauty, Fuscara. The bee becomes an alchemist "Minting the Garden into Gold"; a fortune-teller as, exploring her hand, "He tipples Palmestry and dines / On all her fortune telling lines" (25–26); then "A Proper hawk for such a fist." Later, he becomes a "small familiar" and then a "bold Columbus." And ultimately, if we are to trust Berdan, the bee stings Fuscara out of jealousy. However, the text seems to indicate that the bee, who treats her like "a pretty maze of flowers"—"It is the rose that bleeds when he / Nibbles his nice Phlebotomy"—may not be the same bee that stings her. The lines are unclear at this point, but they read:

> The King of Bees now's jealous grown
> Lest her beams should melt his throne;
> ....
> ....the Envyous Elfe
> Stung her, cause sweeter than himself.
> Sweetness and she are so ally'd
> The *Bee* committed parricide.
>
> (71–82)

There is no useful ambiguity in the lines, though the ambiguity is obvious upon examination. It would seem at first that the King of Bees became jealous and stung Fuscara, but it may be that, after the King of Bees became jealous, the original bee "Errant" turned envious and attacked the living shrine of Flora he had so recently worshipped. In the final analysis, and partly because the ambiguity is plainly of no critical value, Berdan's reading may still be the best and the most obvious. The reference to the King of Bees as if he were a separate character may be nothing more than a way of elevating the status of the original wanderer. Actually, there is no more to be gained from insisting upon this ambiguity as significant than is to be gained from insisting that the last lines of the poem indicate that the bee is in any useful way the offspring of Fuscara. The most felicitous aspect of the final two lines is that they rhyme.

And, truly, this poem has never done well in the hands of modern critics. It is not that this is a poem rich with examples of the excesses of Cleveland's imagery, but it does contain a much-abused line, "Tender as 'twere a Jellie glov'd," which describes Fuscara's hand. Rather, the conceit, after its first freshness, tires quickly. Were the

poem half its length, it would be much more interesting. The first
ten lines, for instance, possess considerable novelty, freshness, and
amusement:

> Natures Confectioner, the *Bee*,
> Whose suckets are moyst *Alchimie*,
> The Still of his refining mould
> Minting the Garden into Gold,
> Having rifled all the fields
> Of what dainties *Flora* yields,
> Ambitious now to take Excise
> Of a more fragrant Paradise,
> At my *Fuscara's* sleeve ariv'd,
> Where all delicious sweets are hiv'd.

If the poet had continued with such imagery and if he had avoided
the temptation to overextension, his poem might have been most
successful. The fact that the poem is overextended leads us to conclude that quite possibly this poem, too, is something of an
exercise—an exercise in the *concetto*. Were it not for the earnest-
ness of the tone of the poem, we might be tempted to conclude that
it is more than just an exercise of the mode, perhaps a parody of it.
Unfortunately, however, we can do nothing more than speculate;
and such speculation is often fruitless. Parody, however, is by no
means out of place in Cleveland's lyrics.

Perhaps for this reason George Kitchin appears confident that
Fuscara is either a burlesque or a parody of the mode of the conceit.
Unfortunately, he offers no evidence beyond his own critical sen-
sitivity. Of Cleveland's poems he says, "Some of his Marinistic productions are obviously genuine. Their absurdity is equaled by their
charm, which is a good test of sincerity."[2] When he deals with *Fuscara*, he offers a cryptic quote from Saintsbury and the first twelve
lines of the poem as his "proof"! Afterward, of course, he admits
that the poem may be sincere and not a parody at all. Thus, like
most critics of Cleveland, Kitchin can offer no stronger proof than
personal conviction to suggest that Cleveland is not serious in his
intention. And—fortunately or unfortunately—until some evidence
comes forth, we must take Cleveland at his word in such poems as
"Fuscara."

CHAPTER 4

"The Political Cleveland"

R UTH Nevo has declared that "political verse as such comes of age with the work of John Cleveland in the 1640's"[1] and, that Cleveland's contemporaries accorded him respect as the first among their poets of politics. This assessment is particularly reasonable in view of the fact that most later poets owe something to Cleveland because he found ways of dealing with political subjects, both appealing and unappealing, which they found congenial and—particularly for Dryden and Butler—which they found useful.

Like many Cambridge poets of the day, Cleveland began his political poetry with an exercise about the Guy Fawkes plot to blow up the king and both Houses of Parliament in 1605. And though it is neither fair nor realistic to measure Cleveland's later achievement by this youthful poem, "On the Pouder Plot" is marked by much the same exuberance and energy that we find in later poems—perhaps because Cleveland, as his editors suggest, revised the poem in later years, or because his youthful energy never left him. In any event, the poem is instructive.

As we have noted, the subject is the Guy Fawkes powder plot of 1605, the attempt to blow up both Houses of Parliament, King James I's personal ministers, and, most important for Cleveland, the king himself. James's situation is likened to that of Charles I in Cleveland's own time, and the lesson the poem teaches is that only grief can befall those who, like the executed Fawkes, threaten the throne.

The similarity with the poem on Edward King is striking. Just as Cleveland declared he could not tolerate "tears in tune," he declares as solemnly in "On the Pouder Plot" that "Satyres run best when Classhing tearms do meet, / And Indignation makes them knock their feet. / To bee methodicall in Verse, & rhime / In sutch inuectiues is the highest crime" (5–8). Naturally, Cleveland goes

blithely ahead and commits the "highest crime" in full knowledge of
the fact that everyone knows he is doing it; but we moderns should
not assume that Cleveland quite meant what he seems to mean. He
does not intend to abandon rhyme, use of metaphor, or metrical
accuracy. True, he begins the poem by declaring he needs no intervention of the muse to help "inspire my quill"; rage, he tells us, will
do nicely. And it is true, as well, that the metrics of a number of the
lines are willfully tortured: line 59, for example, has but one word:
"Then." Instead of abandoning all the normal qualities of verse,
Cleveland intends only to avoid the sleekness which is altogether
possible in the smooth numbers of the lyric poets. On the contrary,
his efforts are to make his satires rough-hewn and thereby more
honest to their inspiration and their subject.

I The Satiric Method

Cleveland gives us every opportunity to discover his own method
in the lines which follow those quoted above from "On the Pouder
Plot":

> Who Euer saw a firy passion breake
> But in abruptnes? thus my pen must speak
> Make at Each word a period, which may show
> As Cornes of pouder, & then fire the row
> With sharp artic'late blasts, which breathing on
> Those lines, may 'nflame each hot expression.
>
> (9–14)

Thus Cleveland is trying to develop his own kind of propriety, but
one of rage—though this word may be too strong for this particular
poem. In his later verse the word "rage," his word for the source of
his inspiration and the name of his muse, is certainly in keeping
with his achievement. The interesting thing is that Cleveland's
muse is rage not only in the political satires but also in the
panegyrics.

It may be fairer to suggest that rage can transform itself in some of
the less caustic poems and become something like sadness or bewilderment. Such seems to be the case in "*Epitaph on the Earl of
Strafford*," a "sonnet" with tetrameter lines which reflects on the
ambiguous position that the once powerful Thomas Wentworth, the
king's chief military advisor during the period of political suppres-
sion known as "Thorough," enjoyed during his lifetime. Strafford

was known to have been fiercely loyal to the king and to have been instructive in advising his sovereign to call the very Parliament which demanded, and got, Strafford's head. King Charles was also said to have been most deeply grieved by his having handed over Strafford to Parliament for execution, for even the king was sensitive to the degree to which Strafford was loyal. Cleveland memorialized him in a touching line: "Here lies Wise and Valiant Dust," and then explored the irony implicit in his having been "The People's violent Love, and Hate." Strafford was indeed in such an ambivalent position through most of his career, and it was not really surprising that he should have submitted himself to a trial and ultimately to an execution which he felt would serve to protect his ruler. As Cleveland says, Strafford was "Huddled up 'twixt Fit and Just," between, in other words, what was necessary and what was right. He served, to his end, the exigencies of his state; and he did so uncomplainingly. Strafford's uncomplaining attitude is the subject of the last lines of the poem and the subject of Cleveland's considerable respect: "Riddles lie here; or in a word, / Here lies Blood; and let it lie / Speechlesse still, and never crie."

The quiet, almost suppressed tone of the poem is what moves anyone familiar with Cleveland's works. When we recall the pyrotechnical elaboration of the poem on Edward King, we cannot help but feel as modern readers that this later, quieter poem is more expressive of a deep feeling. Furthermore, it would seem reasonable to think that the emotion which is so plainly expressed in the poem is not just the result of a response to the death of a single man, but that the emotion is in fact complicated enormously by the implications in political and national terms of the death of this particular man. There is no need to look for personal feelings in the poem or for personal issues, for what the poem talks about is deeper than person. Strafford's death is not a private calamity; it is a public catastrophe.

When Cleveland turned his pen to a very similar subject, the death of Archbishop Laud, the second of the two strong advisors of King Charles, he explains, "The state in *Strafford* fell, the Church in *Laud*" (42); and we may assume that Cleveland was drained of response to such affairs by the time he wrote this poem (it also appeared with the epitaph on Strafford in the 1647, or first, edition of his work). This second execution was much more fully anticipated than the first, and, therefore, the death of the state may simply have been more shocking to Cleveland and to England than the death of the church.

In any case, the poem on the subject of Laud is not marked by the shock and restraint we have seen in the poem on Strafford. Instead, we have more familiar approach to the problem of grief and poetry, an approach seen in the King epitaph and in the poem about Guy Fawkes. A chess player might describe it as a gambit, but a gambit most conspicuously declined:

> I need no Muse to give my passion vent,
> He brews his teares that studies to lament.
> Verse chymically weeps; that pious raine
> Distill'd with Art, is but the sweat o'th'braine.
> Who ever sob'd in numbers?

Such imagery leads us to anticipate another discussion of rainspouts, and we are offered "Not Bushells Wells can match a Poets eyes / In wanton water-works." The imagery, or its force, is quite the same raw stuff that Cleveland worked up to such startling effect in his earlier tribute to Edward King. It sounds prefabricated once we have seen such an elaborate poetic disclaimer used again and again, though in its first use it still has vitality. In the poem to Laud, it sounds pretentious and badly rhetorical, which of course it is; but it also sounds as if Cleveland, in order to work up the poem, had to work up an inflated and false tone of voice. Naturally, this fact is all the more obvious when we have viewed a number of the uses of Cleveland's peculiar convention.

As Saintsbury says of this poem, "If the Strafford epitaph seemed too serious, as well as too concentrated and passionate, for Cleveland, this on Strafford's fellow worker and fellow victim may seem almost a caricature of our author's more wayward and more fantastic manner."[2] Saintsbury praises the poem about Laud for having some good lines in it and for anticipating the style of Dryden, and both observations are quite true. Whether or not the poem itself is an example of the fantastic in Cleveland is something else, for the facts seem to indicate a much simpler kind of case. Cleveland, having succeeded in his poems about King and Guy Fawkes and having established a pattern for the use of the disclaimer, merely continues to use it. Cleveland would have realized that such a disclaimer as "Who ever sob'd in numbers?" would lose its effect with repeated use, and the probability is that he never looked ahead to the time when a number of his poems would appear side by side, as in the 1647 edition, for readers to compare. Had he done so, the chances are he would have been equally rhetorical and mannered, but he would probably have varied his rhetorical stances a good deal.

As it is, the poem on Laud concentrates on hyperbole—all life has been drained from England with Laud's death. In resorting to a technique reminiscent in its intended effect of the epic simile, Cleveland leaves his poem on Strafford far behind. He declares that learning, the church, and the law itself are dead: "There's nothing lives, life is since he is gone, / But a Nocturnall Lucubration" (27— 28). "Death's inventory," Cleveland informs us, when read in the sum total is: *"Canterburie's dead."* And, as if to underscore the injustice of the death of both these men, Cleveland adds, "Be dull great spirits and forbeare to climbe, / For worth is sin and eminence a crime."

Instead of deep lamentation for the death of the man—a quality we do not honestly expect from Cleveland's elegy and one he apparently was not personally interested in investing it with—what we get is anger and vituperation. His muse, in his poem on Laud, is clearly rage; and his energy is used to condemn the public that demanded Laud's death more than it is to lament the fact of that death. What is lamented is the way in which the laws were stretched and pinched in order to ensure the proper outcome of the trials of the "the twins of publike rage." As Cleveland declares, "The facts were done before the Lawes were made, / The trump turn'd up after the game was plai'd" (45–46). As far as Cleveland is concerned, the really lamentable fact is that the laws have died with the death of the state. But such lamentation is not breast-beating; it is not the tearfulness that later ages have come to associate with death.

In the sense that Cleveland uses lamentation, it is another form of outrage. And that emotion is unquestionably genuine, and it is unquestionably present in the majority of the poems that Cleveland wrote about subjects that were of personal importance to him. It is too bad, really, that later critics have demanded an emotional commitment of him that he never intended to make—and one which he never felt he had to make. To have wept over the death of Laud—or of Strafford—would have been personal excess in Cleveland's mind. And his poetry had other work to do than to permit him to give vent to that kind of emotionalizing. As W. R. Parker says in his biography of Milton, death was such an everpresent factor in the lives of all

Christ's College students that it would have been unrealistic to assume that any new, deep emotional reserves would be tapped by each ensuing death. As a recent demographic study of the people of York shows, only 10 percent of the general population lived to age forty in the sixteenth and seventeenth centuries.[3] With death such a commonplace, it is not difficult to see why poets such as Milton would have naturally turned to conventional forms to help give form and meaning to grief. The pastoral forms of *Epitaphium Damonis*, written for, young Diodati, the best friend Milton had, and *Lycidas*, for King, do not belie emotion; they give it shape. Such is the case, too, with Cleveland and his use of wit as an expression of grief and his use of outrage as a general expression of emotion.

II *"Rupertismus": Political Venom*

At 180 lines, "To P. Rupert"—or "Rupertismus" as the poem was earlier titled—is one of Cleveland's most ambitious, nonsatiric polit-ical poems. Rupert was the dashing young military hero on whom Charles I had pinned his hopes for a quick defeat of Parliamentary troops. Rupert, Charles's nephew (recalling the traditional heroic relationship of Beowulf to Hygelac and Gawain to King Arthur), was a formidable hero even before he set foot in England. Cleveland has many opportunities for witty invention both in praising Rupert and in ridiculing his enemies, but the poem does not express the kind of sustained outrage which characterizes Cleveland's poem on Laud, nor does it reflect the kind of shock which seems clearly expressed in the epitaph on Strafford. Rather, a mixture of contempt and irritation is expressed against the Roundheads and Parliamentarian sympathizers—not to mention the leaders of Parliament, like John Pym, Sir John Glynne, and Sir John Maynard—as well as a liberal measure of awe and respect for Rupert's posture and his achieve-ment. This poem was probably written during the earliest years of the war, possibly as early as 1642, when things were going relatively well for the king and before anyone, as Saintsbury says, "found out [Rupert's] fatal defects as a general."[4]

At this point in history, Rupert was thought to be a deliverer from abroad, a dashing and invincible model of the perfect cavalier; and from these very qualities stemmed, of course, his defects. He at first was most successful because the Parliamentarian armies were at first most insecure; however, Rupert failed later, at Marston Moor in 1644, even before Cromwell and the New Model Army (an army built on the strength of zeal and discipline) brought him a serious and skilled variety of opponents. But Rupert touched something very deep in the hearts of those Englishmen who saw in him the apotheosis of the hero. He was the outlander nephew of the king; and he was thus the youthful and warlike champion of the king's cause in the ancient and honored forms of the heroic modes that Cromwell's zealots outmoded. Unlike Beowulf, Prince Rupert could not undo Grendel, and never had the chance to face his Dam; the foreign prince turned out to be no deliverer.

But, when Cleveland wrote his poem, Rupert was particularly notable for his having slashed into the midst of battles with not the slightest scratch accruing to his person. As Cleveland says, "But you're enchanted, Sir; you're doubly free / From the great Guns and squibbing Poetrie: / Whom neither Bilbo nor Invention pierces, / Proofe even 'gainst th' Artillerie of Verses" (29–32). Of course the second of the threats, the "keen iambics" of rebel poets, is more the subject of Cleveland's poem than the first, the Balboa ("Bilbo") steel of Puritan swords. What Cleveland implies throughout the early part of the poem is that the "Language of the dayes" (15) is such that reading a poem must be done "with Hebrew Spectacles; / Interpret Counter, what is Crosse rehears'd" (24–25); in other words, a poem must be treated as saying the reverse of what it says. And for this reason Cleveland begins his own poem with a rhetorical disclaimer: "O that I could but vote my selfe a Poet!" in the manner of the Parliament, which notoriously had the "Legislative knacke to do it!" and much more besides.

Such discussion is amusing in its own way, but the main texture of the poem is such that the modern reader is likely to find the interpretation difficult, even with the illuminations of three editors; without them, however, he would find the poem impossible. As Saintsbury suggested, deciphering *"To P. Rupert"* requires a good deal of "scholiastry." Even with that, however, the rewards are slim. We do not thrill as much today to references such as, *"Wharton* tell his Gossops of the City / That you kill women too" (42–43), as the original readers apparently did. This poem suffers from what all such highly topical poems suffer from: we do not know Wharton, an early advocate of Parliament's position, and a minor Baron whose principal claim to fame was his having delivered a number of speeches describing battles in which things had gone poorly for his own men and well for Prince "Robert." In these speeches he has

cause to accuse the Royalist leader of killing men, their oxen, and
their women and children. This accusation was most hotly contested
in print, and Cleveland considers it worthy of satirical reply. But
even knowing all this does not revitalize the imagery for us; it still
remains a bit of historical hardware.

Cleveland seems to have given some thought to the probability
that such poetry would age rapidly; and, in all fairness to what he is
able to accomplish in his poem on Rupert, we must admit that in
comparison with other poems of the day which try much the same
thing, "To P. Rupert" is still somewhat amusing, even without the
scholarly research necessary to have command of each and every
detail. (Of course, most of the materials are readily available, as I
have indicated, for any reader of the notes to the several editions.)
But Cleveland can manage at times to use the contemporary allusions, which he mixes with a light load of classical references, with
enough skill for them to still function as he wanted them to.
Saintsbury points out the curious center portion of the poem, which
devotes much of its attention to Boy, Prince Rupert's dog and his
suspected "familiar." In Boy, Cleveland sees a chance at some lasting witty invention:

> they fear
> Even his Dog, that four-legg'd *Cavalier:*
> He that devoures the scraps, which *Lundsford* makes,
> Whose picture feeds upon a child in stakes:
> Who name but *Charles*, hee comes aloft for him,
> But holds up his Malignant leg at *Pym.*
>
> (121–26)

The last line is a most deliciously turned Clevelandism and is one
much admired by later wits.

The imagery which Cleveland attaches to Boy is inventive but it is
also quite standardly developed and applied. Cleveland uses a
catalog to list the several qualities of interest to him. He sets it up by
declaring that Parliament has a number of "Articles" against him:
"First, that he barks against the sense o' the House" (128), which is
to say that Boy himself has more sense than the House has. The
second charge against him is "his ceremonious wag o' the taile," an
obscure allusion which probably satirizes Parliament's ability to find
a lapse in religious orthodoxy even in the wag of a dog's tail. Cleveland compounds the image with a reference to a "Countess

. . . *Lust's Amsterdam,* / That lets in all religious of the game" (133–34). The countess has been tentatively identified by Saintsbury as Lucy, Countess of Carlisle, a traitress and a wanton ("Amsterdam" being synonomous for "free-thinking"); therefore, Boy could expect to be let off lightly on this charge if he could get the Countess to stand his "Baile."

The third charge against Boy is that he is quicker to smell "Intelligence" than Pym, who was noted for setting his own plots and "intelligencing" them himself. The final charge involves not religion or politics, but magic. An obscure "charge" in many ways—not discussed by any of the editors—it suggests an "in" joke or reference to a heraldic pedigree: perhaps a mock-heraldry that Cleveland works up for the feared and spritely little dog himself: "Lastly, he is a Devill without doubt: / For when he would lie downe, he wheels about, / Makes circles, and is couchant in a ring; / And therefore score up one for conjuring" (139–42).

This catalog of charges leads to a most amusing response on the part of Boy and to an example of Cleveland's ability to simulate the real energies of direct address:

> O Quarter, quarter!
> I'me but an Instrument, a meer Sir *Arthur.*
> If I must hang, ô let not our fates varie,
> Whose office 'tis alike to fetch and carry.
> No hopes of a reprieve, the mutinous stir
> That strung the Jesuite, will dispatch a cur.
> Were I a Devill as the Rabble feares,
> I see the House would try me by my Peeres.
>
> (143–50)

The Sir Arthur in question is possibly Sir Arthur Haselrig, an unimportant instrument of the state; and, though the reference to "the Jesuite" may be a particular reference to a particular hanging, the chances are that it is merely a generic reference indicating that any rabble that would hang a Catholic would just as easily hang a dog. The last lines hit home with no need for a gloss. The entire passage devoted to Boy is an exercise in mock-heroic, and a stimulating one at that. Naturally, it plays on the current suspicion that Boy was a "familiar" capable of great magical powers and was responsible, ultimately, for Prince Rupert's uncanny ability to go unscathed through the hail of arms and poems.

However, Cleveland does not leave the poem at the point which seems almost to approve the popular notion of Rupert's powers being dependent on the spirit of his dog. Rather, Cleveland embarks on one of his "enormous and disgusting hyperboles" in order to emphasize that Rupert himself is the power the rabble fears. Cleveland comes dangerously close to blaspheming in his invocation of St. Peter and Jove, and in such lines as "Your name can scare an Athiest to his prayers" (173) Cleveland even makes a remarkable connection between Jove's begetting of Perseus in the shower of gold which falls in Danae's lap and the divine protection which Rupert enjoyed:[5] "Sure *Iove* descended in a leaden shower / To get this *Perseus:* hence the fatall power / Of shot is strangled: bullets thus allied, / Feare to commit an act of Parricide" (161–64).

There are many problems with this imagery. To begin with, the catachretic elements which make this a likely Clevelandism, according to Dryden's standards, force us to treat the entire conceit with caution. It simply does not work in its entirety, though those elements which do work are ingenious. What works is the surprise of the shower of gold likened to the shower of lead: both are beneficent to the chosen hero because both are sent by Jove himself. But for this very reason the showers have their problems. Jove cannot be delivering the Parliament's shot and shell, nor is the rebel shower of lead producing any offspring: it is not being dropped in Danae's lap, or in the lap of a woman; it is hailing upon the Perseus in question, Rupert himself. The image depends on our willingness to take the connections between the two heavy metals raining from above (the sky-god Jove) with the gold being heavenly and with the lead being mundane or worse (it comes from Parliament) and then not pressing further beyond its obvious limits.

Such imagery was too much for a critic like Johnson, though it may not be too much for a critic who reads the conceits of John Donne, Andrew Marvell, and Abraham Cowley with a sympathetic eye. Like all conceits, Cleveland's is highly unlikely at first glance, then on second though it is striking in its applicability—if only on a limited basis. This image is notable in that the failure of the connection between the shower of gold and the shower of lead seems to grow in our understanding much faster than the success of the connection; in other words, after the initial surprise and delight comes a reflection which reveals that Cleveland is satisfying himself with a relatively superficial comparison. What he is aiming at is an explanation of Rupert's ability to stand the rain of "Cannons" that "doe but lisp and complement" him rather than kill him. Jove's protection, as of old, is responsible.

But Cleveland continues to work with the concept of a Rupert who enjoys divine protection and who, almost Christlike, shares the powers of divinity. He mixes elements with considerable abandon, relying not only on the relationship of divinity to Rupert but also on the suggestion of magic developed in the discussion of Boy. Rupert's name alone becomes something to regard, and it enjoys the same magical power that the names of divines (and devils) enjoy:

> Your name can scare an Athiest to his prayers;
> And cure the Chin-cough better then the bears.
> Old *Sybill* charmes the Tooth-ach with you: Nurse
> Makes you still children; nay and the pond'rous curse
> The Clownes salute with, is deriv'd from you;
> (*Now Rupert take thee, Rogue;* how dost thou do?)
>
> (173–78)

Complimentary as these lines are, there is still the suggestion that Rupert's great powers are being wasted on trivialities. But, if his powers are so pervasive as to be brought to the masses, as Cleveland suggests they are, we must put up with the uses that "Nurses" and "Athiests" and "Clownes" can conceive for such divine influence. Nonetheless, the modernization of "Devil take thee" comes as something of a comic surprise, since it is unlikely that Cleveland wishes us to think of Rupert as a mere devil.

III   Eclipsing Both King and Cause

Times changed, of course; and by 1645 the aura of splendor which had surrounded Rupert was shattered. Cromwell's New Model Army crushed Rupert at Naseby on June 14 after Rupert overextended his cavalry in what appeared initially to be a brilliant act of daring. Actually a bit of flamboyancy, it caught up with Rupert and the entire cause. Cleveland's poem *"The General Eclipse"* expresses in seven five-line stanzas and in what is perhaps an overly lyric fashion some of the dismay at the loss of not only the cause, but all of the color, the brightness, and the glamour of the age of the cavalier. The poem is light and almost silly in face of the significance of the events (which may be more cause for justifying Morris and Withington's inclusion of the poem under "probable poems"). But superficial or not, some of the images of this poem figure quite prominently in what must be treated as a genuine Cleveland poem in all senses: *The Kings Disguise.*"

In *"The General Eclipse,"* Cleveland works with light and dark
• imagery which sees development later:

> Ladies that guild the glittering Noon,
> And by Reflection mend his Ray,
> Whose Beauty makes the sprightly Sun
> To dance, as upon Easter-day;
>   What are you now the Queen's away?
>
> Courageous Eagles, who have whet
> Your eyes upon Majestick Light,
> And thence deriv'd such Martial heat,
> That still your Looks maintain the Fight;
>   What are you since the King's Goodnight?

> (1–10)

The imagery of the eagle, the sun, and the darkening of the eclipse figure prominently in his poem on Charles. And, more than that, the imagery which receives tentative treatment in *"The General Eclipse"* is greatly expanded later: the religious imagery associated with the reference to the eagle looking upon "Majestick Light" is an image which refers to the medieval assumption that the eagle was the only bird who could look at the sun, just as St. John was the only apostle who could look on the face of God. Those who were in the presence of the king were all eagles—all blessed with looking on the light which emanated from majesty.

In this lyric treatment, such imagery does not have a chance to build or to develop any profundity of meaning. But, in the poem on King Charles's flight to the Scots, the imagery has more room, more chances for exploring implications. This poem is by one who still wants to "maintain the Fight" but who feels eerily deserted by the very one who gave the fight meaning: the king himself. As Morris and Withington say, this poem is probably "Cleveland's most bitter, despairing work."[6] But beyond despair—perhaps because of it—the poem is marked by the most remarkable statement and profession of faith found in Cleveland's poems. The poem is almost bald in the sense that it is an exercise in paradox, an effort to explore every possibility for the failure of human understanding to accommodate a situation which seemed so unreasonable as to virtually constitute a godlike effort to confound mankind.

What Cleveland resorts to, at last, is faith itself—faith in his king which resembles faith in God. Cleveland's only way out, the only way to avoid despair, the only way to explain the unexplainable, is faith. It is the alternative he has to renouncing a king who has seemed to renounce himself. Cleveland sees in the king's action something of the grandeur of Christ's offering himself on the cross, but in actuality the king's motives were anything but so glorious as that. It is particularly interesting that Cleveland should resort to this virtually godlike faith as a last resort since—if we keep in mind just how secular a poet he is—few references of a religious sort are found in his poems. Because he finally resorts to such faith, we appreciate the real meaning of his desperation.

What happened was that the king, in April of 1646, realized that all was over for him. Cleveland, as the chief officer at Newark, had held on under Leslie's siege until the king himself commanded him to turn the garrison over to the enemy on May 6 or 7, after he had himself surrendered to the Scots. But on April 27, just before Parliament began the siege of the king's headquarters at Oxford, Charles assumed a disguise and slipped away to wander about the surrounding countryside for eight days until, on May 5, he decided to give himself up to the Scots near the very spot where Cleveland had surrendered. His intentions were to avoid putting himself in the hands of Parliament, and he thought he could treat with the Scots. But his intentions were never realized, and he was ultimately turned over to the Parliament, which beheaded him in 1649. At the time in which Cleveland writes—the year 1646, immediately after the king had assumed his disguise and fled, the fatal conclusion of the king's affairs was thought likely. What Cleveland is expressing is his total dismay at the failure of his cause and at the denigration of his king.

The poem plays with blindness, darkness, even the concept (which seems to have peculiarly fascinated him in other poems) of negritude, as in such lines as: "Nor bodily nor ghostly Negro could / Rough-cast thy figure in a sadder mould" (21–22). The poem also plays with the concept of brightness and brilliance, and particularly with the sun's light and with its bizarre and unnatural eclipse: "The Sun wears Midnight, Day is Beetle-brow'd, / And Lightning is in Keldar of a cloud" (45–46). As these lines indicate, the poem is also deeply sensitive to the fact that essences are beclouded by forms and by outward shapes—by, in many cases, nothing but the obfuscation of clothing "And three-pil'd darkness" (56). The very fact that such a magnificence as the king could be so totally obscured by a mere disguise (though it is, as he says, no "filme of tiffany ayre, / No Cob-web vizard" [51–52]) overwhelms Cleveland, but it also gives him his way out in the poem. Since it is plain that "*Charles* and his Maske are of a different mint" (43), "Y' are not i' th' presence, though the King be there" (70). Things, then, are not what they seem; and even Cleveland needs "Keyes for this Cypher" (109), keys which would unlock

> This Cabinet, whose aspect would benight
> Critick spectators with redundant light.
> A Prince most seen, is least: What Scriptures call
> The Revelation, is most mysticall.
>   Mount then thou shadow royall, and with haste
> Advance thy morning star, *Charles's* overcast.
> May thy strange journey contradictions twist,
> And force faire weather from a Scottish mist.
>
>   (111–18)

And, ultimately, he must be content to take it on faith, trust, and hope that in the end all will be for the good and that the Scottish mist will prove Mosaic and "Thus *Israel*-like he travells with a cloud, / Both as a Conduct to him, and a shroud" (121–22). And this last, odd suggestion of death brings us to another theme of importance, a theme that actually opens the poem in line 1: "And why so coffin'd in this vile disguise." The disguise, the eclipse, the dimming of the brilliant tide of monarchy equal a demi-death.

There is something uncannily prophetic about this particular imagery; and it may be pertinent to mention that Cleveland has gained a reputation as a seer in connection with the king's ultimate fate. At least one of his early biographers mentions that Cleveland some three days before the king's surrender "foresaw" pieces of silver on the banks of the Tweed, representing the betrayal of his prince.[7] The complex nature of the betrayal, however, was probably never fully appreciated by Cleveland. He was relatively certain that the Scots, to whom the king surrendered purposefully, would betray him; and they did. But he was probably not so fully prepared to believe that the king would betray himself and his own cause. In some senses *"The Kings Disguise"* is a poem which tries, perhaps unsuccessfully, to come to some understanding of the king's own self-betrayal—particularly his willingness to obscure himself, to appear to be something other than what he, in fact, was. As Cleveland powerfully puts it:

> Oh the accurst Stenographie of fate!
> The Princely Eagle shrunke into a Bat.
> What charme, what Magick vapour can it be
> That checkes his rayes to this Apostasie?
>
> (47–50)

The imagery, particularly at this point in the poem, is of considerable force; and it is a compelling expression of Cleveland's bewilderment.

The tone of the poem is reminiscent of Cleveland's epitaph for Strafford in that the immensity of the situation has struck him—though possibly not with the clarity of things relative to Strafford—and Cleveland's responses are profound, if somewhat confused. If it is true that Cleveland was sensitive not only to the impending betrayal but also to the impending death of the king, then it must have been an astonishing thing for him to contemplate, after the death of the state and death of the church, the death of the monarch. Such a circumstance could be likened only to the very death of God.

Probably because of his effort to express his feelings about such an enormity, Cleveland resorts to such extensive use of religious imagery. Not only does he employ those images already discussed, but he resorts also to the details appropriate to a monkish disguise and therefore to details relative to the destruction and desecration of the churches (a practice of the Puritans) and particularly of university chapels. But the irony, of course, is that what a "usurper" would do to the king, if he had him in his power, the king has already done: "What an usurper to his Prince is wont, / Cloyster and shave him, he himselfe hath don't. / His muffled fabrick speakes him a recluse, / His ruines prove it a religous house" (7–10). And merging the prevalent bird imagery (as in "The Sun hath mew'd his beames" [11]) with the religious imagery of the monastery, Cleveland develops: "Like to a martyr'd Abbeys courser doome, / Devoutly alter'd to a Pigeon roome . . . Or if there be a prophanation higher, / Such is the Sacriledge of thine Attire" (29–34). Then, ultimately, the king becomes

"Angell of light, and darknesse too, I doubt, / Inspir'd within, and yet posses'd without. / Majestick twilight in the state of grace, / Yet with an excommunicated face" (39–42).

Perhaps it is noteworthy that Cleveland does not explore the clenches which are prominent in line 41 ("Majestick twilight in the state of grace") but merely sets them there for us to consider. The tone of the quatrain is such that the puns do not demand expansion and do not seem the principal focus of the passage. More striking is the implication of the king's being an angel both of light and darkness, and this ambiguity may be the root of the poem's basic ambiguity.

Ambiguity is the very core of the poem. And Cleveland's position in regard to the ambiguity is peculiar: he has not fully resolved the problems he perceives and develops in terms of highly suggestive imagery. He is hopeful, yet not totally convinced, that what has happened will in the end be good. As he says in the most hopeful lines of the poem: "Me thinks in this your dark mysterious dresse / I see the Gospell coucht in Parables" (93–94). But the ambiguity of his treatment of the king is such that we do not become convinced, even when Cleveland himself may seem to be convinced. As modernists we tend to overvalue ambiguities—they seem to offer literary riches where otherwise there would be the poverty of declamation—but we also have learned to respect the artistry essential to balancing ambiguities without their becoming merely parallel and alternative positions. *"The Kings Disguise"* succeeds not only as Cleveland's bitterest poem but also as one of his richest—and it is one of his best because he is able to conceive and elaborate the ambiguities he does. They torture him, and they provide the focus for one of his most intensely focused poems.

A final note to this poem could profitably call attention to peculiarities in the rhyming of certain lines. For one thing, there is a pronounced ambiguity about some of the rhymes. The last couplet cited above is one of the strangest of all, rhyming "dresse" with "Parables." The lines themselves are perfectly regular five-foot iambics, but the rhymes are remarkably ill-suited. The poem has many more rhymes which are questionable—though doubtless much less so in Cleveland's day than our own—but there are some which were probably as unlikely then as now. A few are: "haste"-"overcast" (115–16); "end"-"fiend" (79–80) [though "end"-"friend"]; "rabble"-"stable" (31–32); "could"-"mould" (21–22).[8] They may be of little overall importance in the poem, but I suspect they may be something of a clue to the straining Cleveland underwent not only in the composition of the poem but in the working out of the central ambiguities.

The range, then, of these primarily nonsatirical political poems is quite remarkable. Cleveland in his own time was more famous for his satirical poems, and he is still justly more famed for his exercises in satire; but he should not be overlooked as a poet capable of direct political statement. His muse was sometimes justly rage and sometimes merely bewilderment, but he always seemed aware of the meaning of events and of the portent of change.

CHAPTER 5

The Satiric Strain

FOR a time, Cleveland was thought to be the first to invent the English style of satire, in which people, not just institutions, were attacked, and in which the attack was couched in very specific rather than very general terms.[1] This claim to priority is no longer recognized, but the fact remains that Cleveland set a style, through his own enormous popularity, of satirical attack which became the vogue of the Restoration and early eighteenth-century satirists. Rather than concentrate on the constructive uses of satire as a means of calling attention to shortcomings which, when attended to, could be eliminated, Cleveland concentrated on developing a satire that was a weapon. Just as the ball and shell have few constructive purposes, the satire in the hands of Cleveland is a mode of attack, exposing the subjects' flank and rear to as much elegant abuse as Cleveland's mastery of invention permitted.

Cleveland's success was so great that he was, in turn, attacked violently by the Parliamentarians; but, since he was himself developing a mode which had only been nascent before him, he clearly had the advantage and swept the field. His war was not against flesh, but feeling; it was a wholesale onslaught on the self-respect of his adversary, and he proved that his adversary was indeed thin-skinned and perhaps insecure. The Royalists delighted in his character of the Parliamentarians and their institutions; for, to the Royalists, such attacks represented, as the war progressed, their only genuine successes. Cleveland's "keen iambics" were indeed biting, and they stirred both sides of the conflict so greatly that Cleveland himself must, at times, have been surprised. As C. V. Wedgwood observed, Cleveland's satirical verse was "the most bitter that the Civil War produced," and it was "a tribute to his reputation as the most deadly and skilful of the Cavalier satirists."[2]

I   *Satire: The Topical Art*

One of the reasons for his having been so successful, apart from the novelty of his style of personal attack, was the fact—as Wedgwood also notes—that Cleveland was the most relentlessly topical of the Cavalier poets. For this reason, as is true in his political verse, the satires are difficult for us to appreciate today; for the wit that was once merely embedded in them is, in great part, now buried. The topical poet usually pays for his contemporary success, should he be fortunate enough to enjoy it, with later obscurity. The reasons are fairly obvious: we no longer recognize the people, events, or circumstances which form the subject of the poems; and, even if we do recognize some of them, the times are such that we no longer care about them.

The subjects of Cleveland's satires were among the most important ones of his day. His most celebrated satire, and probably his best-known poem, is on the general subject of the Scots, unquestionably the most important deciding factor in the Civil War. But Cleveland also wrote about less immediately pressing things. His subjects include an attack on the Westminster Assembly, the gathering of divines who sought to fix the new modes of English worship; on the infamous "etcetera" oath; and on the "Smectymnuuns," the five divines whose writings, having been roasted in the pamphlet wars by Bishop Hall, the eminent character writer, were defended by Milton in his "Apology for Smectymnuus." In all of these subjects, Cleveland's audience would have seen issues of importance which impinged directly on their own expression of personal liberty. They would have seen, as well, portraits or characters of both types and individuals which they could recognize (and verify) from their own personal experience. Such recognition was much of the charm of many of these satires for Cleveland's audience; and, if we are to judge by *Hudibras* and by Dryden's later satires, Cleveland provided the model for the satire of the next age.

Typical, in certain limited ways, of Cleveland's general approach to satire on political and religious affairs is his poem on the "etcetera" oath, "*A Dialogue between two Zealots, upon the &c. in the Oath.*" The poem, sixty-two couplet lines long, was much enjoyed and much reprinted. It appeared in the 1647 edition of the collected Cleveland, but it also appeared earlier, in an unreliable version, in *The Decoy Duck: Together with the Discovery of the Knot in the Dragons Tayle calld &c.* (1642), as well as in a number of collections after 1647. The poem may have been written and read by a small audience as early as 1640. Such a possibility is interesting since, while the poem is typical of Cleveland's satires in its amusing portraits and its having attacked such a "hot" issue, it is obviously a poem in an early style. It is too gentle, too comfortably amusing, and too light in touch to be a late poem. It has none of the relentless invective, none of the ruthless and brutal attack which characterize the later poems. For Cleveland, the zealots were not be be taken very seriously; they were feckless and amusing but surely not the threat they were soon to become.

The "etcetera" oath, a peculiar document, was designed to secure the allegiance of all divines to the present system of church government. It was formulated at difficult time just after the Scots had bound themselves by a "Solemn League and Covenant" to resist by force if necessary any tampering with their Kirk by the edicts of Archbishop Laud.[3] The oath was formulated after the first Bishops' War, in which Scotland showed it was not only willing to resist but was thoroughly capable of resistance. Cleveland and most Anglicans, unaware of the seriousness of events, thought the oath quite harmless; they could not understand the resentment and alarm which came from, particularly, the Independents. The oath sought to secure church government by bishops, thus also ensuring, as if echoing James I's Hampton Court declaration of "No bishop, no king," the stability not only of the church, but of King Charles's government.

The oath, to be sworn to by all schoolmasters, divines, and people of importance connected with the church, read thus:

I, A. B., do swear that I do approve the doctrine and discipline, or government, established in the Church of England, as containing all things necessary to salvation, and that I will not endeavour by myself or any other, directly or indirectly, to bring in Popish doctrine, contrary to that which is so established, nor will I ever give my consent to alter the government of the Church by archbishops, bishops, deans, and archdeacons, &c., as it stands now established, and as by right it ought to stand, nor yet ever to subject it to the usurpations and superstitions of the See of Rome.

This document represented a painfully obvious "last ditch" effort to resist the forces of change which threatened the church on all sides, just as it was a painfully obvious move on Archbishop Laud's part to guarantee himself the security of his office.

The oath was one more offense against Presbyterians, Independents, and any others seeking reform of church government. And, while good Anglicans and monarchists such as Cleveland could see no harm in it, those who took offense were offended deeply and found in the bravado of the ampersand, "&c.," which appeared not only in the oath, but in Cleveland's poem (though Berdan prints "etcetera"), a tail by which the whole structure of church and state could be shaken. Cleveland puns on the ampersand in many ways; but in his amusement he also demonstrates his wit and his ability to outdo all those who attacked the "etcetera" oath by going them more than just one better. The principal focus of his satire is on Sir Roger and his fellow zealot, both comically ranting Puritans whose total text is "&c."

But beyond that principal focus is the remarkable *tour de force* of their attack on the oath; and, if it were not for the fact that the zealots drink themselves in "liquid Oath" until "they and their Tribe were all &c" (62), as the last line of the poem says, we might almost be tempted to think Cleveland was sympathetic with their cause. The only other clue to the fact that he is satirical about their complaints is the enormous epic inflation of the ampersand, particularly amusing in such lines as, "Yet here's not all, I cannot halfe untruss / &c. it's so abdominous. / The *Trojan* Nag was not so fully lin'd" (43–45). Such inflation was Cleveland's stock-in-trade, and its employment alone is no guarantee of his intentions.

His intentions in this poem are made clear from the first lines on: "Sir *Roger*, from a zealous piece of Freeze, / Rais'd to a Vicar of the Childrens threes," is uncompromisingly slanderous. The first line identifies this Roger as a divine ("Sir"), a Puritan ("zealous"), and an impoverished nobody ("Freeze," an allusion to the cheap frieze coats sometimes worn by students). The second line, however, is a puzzle. Even Saintsbury says, "I have been waiting a long time to know what 'children's threes' means."[4] Later editors have not clarified the line, but it seems to refer to some legal distribution of property from a will. Cleveland was quite likely at the Law Line at Cambridge when this poem was written, and the term is probably related to his concerns at the time. Its meaning may well be nothing more than a suggestion that Sir Roger is a most petty "Vicar," since the legal term refers to the third portion of the estate which by law passes to the children, who in turn divide it among themselves until what once was substantial is made inconsequential. The annual sal-

ary, less "Vailes," or extras, would bear this out, since "twenty
Nobles" amounted to less than seven pounds, a minor living at best.

Once the slander is established, "the same Clergie Elfe" disputes
"with a Brother of the Cloth" about "a strange mis-shapen Monster,
/ &c.," which they see as "a neast / Of young *Apocryphaes*," but
which Cleveland sees as merely the "fashion / Of a new mentall
Reservation" (14–16). Once they join in beating the oath, they become prime targets for some broad and subtle satire. One of the
most amusing passages in the poem taunts the zealots about their
treatment of the Bible:

> While *Roger* thus divides the Text, the other
> Winks and expounds, saying, My pious Brother,
> Hearken with reverence; for the point is nice,
> I never read on't, but I fasted twice,
> And so by Revelation know it better
> Then all the learn'd Idolaters o' the' Letter,
>
> (17–22)

The humor depends on our knowing that the Puritans were given to
relying solely on the text of the Bible in their sermons, but some of
them certainly did not read it well, in which case (often, in any case)
they determined the truth by revelation and inner light. The reference to Sir Roger's dividing the text is a delightful poke at the
Puritan divines' frequent practice of dichotomizing in the Ramist
manner the points of either a text or a sermon.[5] This passage is
marvelously humorous in light of the peculiar difficulties the Ramist
would have in dichotomizing "&c."

In the hands of the fasting, unlettered Brother, the ampersand
becomes amplified virtually beyond recognition, which was a complaint the Anglicans had against those who took issue with a mere
"etcetera": they inflated it beyond all proportion. Of course, the
Brother swells himself into a Goliath (24) to deal with the theme;
and he strikes out at once to declare the "&c" to be the "curled locke
of Antichrist" (26). And from that it grows through various stages
until it becomes "the darke Vault wherein th' infernall plot / Of
powder 'gainst the State was first begot" (37–38); but, at the end of
the sermon, the Brother lapses into the vernacular, saying, "&c.
will be too farre to sweare: / For 'tis (to speake in a familiar stile) / A
Yorkshire Wea-bit, longer then a mile" (50–52).

In response to his Brother's sermonizing virtuosity, Sir Roger swears blasphemously and settles down to a blasphemous liquid oath ("bloody wine, / He swears shall seal the Synods *Cataline*" [57–58]), which he does not forego until his "eleventh quart." The two of them, naturally, drink themselves out of the question and become, for the reader, ridiculous rather than disturbing.

II *The Puritan as Hypocrite*

This effect is also achieved in another portrait of the Puritan as hypocrite and licentiate in "*Square-Cap*," which is comprised of six eight-line stanzas which ridicule Puritan headgear:

> Next comes the Puritan in a *wrought-Cap*,
> With a long-wasted conscience towards a Sister,
> And making a Chappell of Ease of her lap,
> First he said grace, and then he kist her.
> Beloved, quoth he, thou art my Text,
> Then falls he to Use and Application next:
>> But then she replied, your Text (Sir) I'le be,
>> For then I'm sure you'l ne'r handle me.
>
> (24–31)

Here, the Puritan is merely a rogue, and our delight in the lines comes from our perception of the contradictory (catachretic) nature of his behavior, given his principles and given the imagery of conscience, chapel, prayer, and text. "*Square-Cap*" is a light, amusing poem which is probably as early as, and possibly earlier than, the "Dialogue." The range of probability, according to Cleveland's editors, is from 1643–1647, but the poem was first printed in the fifth edition of the works in 1647. The picture of the Puritan as a simple and amusing hypocrite marks this as an early effort.

But in "The Hue and Cry After Sir John Presbyter," we have an entirely different situation. We have a description of the Puritans which does not emphasize their ludicrousness so much as their dangerous "*Antick* heads." The poem is sixty lines of venom and rage, but it is controlled in such a way as to help us understand that now Cleveland is taking the Puritans seriously and that his description of them must be read closely. This is a later poem, one which internal evidence—the reference to "The *Negative* and *Covenanting* Oath" (7)—marks as having been written after early 1646. By this time, Rupert had been defeated; the king had surrendered to the Scots; the war was, for all intents and purposes, over; and the league of Presbyterians and Puritans had gathered to draw up plans for the proper modes of worship in the Westminster Assembly. There was no reason to treat lightly the threat to individual religious liberty, and there was no longer any justification for portraying the opposition as simple-minded and feckless. The decrees of the Westminster Assembly would become binding by law and would affect all Englishmen, just as Archbishop Laud's decrees would have become law and would have affected all Scotsmen. Now, of course, the shoe was indeed on the other foot; and the first step taken was to offend more Englishmen than just the Royalists.

As a Royalist, and particularly now as a defeated one, Cleveland takes "Sir John Presbyter" very seriously. His mixture of religious and military imagery in the opening lines of the poem shows just what he thinks of those men who sat peacefully, under protection of Cromwell's muskets, to outline the proper ways for all Englishmen to pray:

> With Hair in Characters, and Lugs in text;
> With a splay mouth, & a nose circumflext;
> With a set Ruff of Musket bore, that wears
> Like Cartrages or linen Bandileers,
> Exhausted of their sulpherous Contents
> In Pulpit fire-works, which that Bomball vents;
>
> (1–6)

After the normal abuse of person and the description of big ears (lugs), short hair, broad mouth, and twisted nose, Cleveland describes Sir John's neck-ruff as if it were a hellish row of empty cartridges. This description is witty and appropriate but not funny.

None of this poem could properly be called funny; its seriousness, as a satire, is its most remarkable characteristic. As Saintsbury and others have pointed out, Cleveland is attacking the Westminster Assembly's ordinances with a seriousness that is matched by Milton's in his caudal sonnet on the "new forcers of conscience." The fact that Cleveland and Milton are on different sides of the conflict is less important than the fact that both react badly to being told what their forms of worship will be. As Milton says, "New Presbyter is but Old Priest writ large." Cleveland reacts against the Assembly's *"Divine right* of an *Ordinance,"* and attacks "These new *Exchange-men* of *Religion"* (34) with what is virtually a humorless intensity. Cleveland sees what Milton does: "Then what Imperious in the Bishop sounds. / The same the *Scotch* Executor rebounds" (39–40). This irony the men in power neither recognized nor appreciated; and it is possibly just as ironic that these former schoolfellows should both have appreciated it themselves in 1646. The utter seriousness of Cleveland's views dominates the last portion of the poem, which treats the Assembly as a group of philistines:

> *Downe* Dagon Synod *with thy motley ware,*
> *Whilst we doe swagger for the* Common-Prayer;
> *That Dove-like Embassie, that wings our sence*
> *To Heavens gate in shape of innocence.*
> *Pray for the Miter'd Authors, and Defie*
> *These* Demicasters *of Divinitie.*

> (53–58)

And thus, by comparison, the bishops and their Common Prayer seem not merely harmless but virtually a tonic.

"Upon Sir Thomas Martin," almost certainly written shortly after March 27, 1643, falls fairly much between the polarities of the early and late treatments by Cleveland of the Puritans. The subject is really quite serious, that of sequestration; and the treatment of Sir Thomas is a fine example of the skill Cleveland brought to the writing of characters. In March, 1643, when Parliament passed an ordinance designed to raise money for pursuing the war, the ordinance provided for the sequestration, or commandeering, of the properties of all those who opposed Parliament in thought (allegiance) or deed (bearing arms). The intentions of Parliament were primarily directed at securing the lands of bishops and other wealthy and influential churchmen, but the implications were clear: this ordinance could be used against all those who stood against Parliament. The fact is, too, that Cleveland's own father had his estate sequestered and was fighting through the courts as late as 1652; but he eventually won in his effort to retain his holdings. Of course, it is doubtful that Cleveland looked ahead to the time when his own family would be involved in a sequestration suit, but he did attack Martin with a lasting anger.

Ostensibly, the attack is less about threats of sequestration than about abuse of privilege. The extended title of the poem explains: "Upon Sir Thomas Martin, Who subscribed a Warrant thus: *We the Knights and Gentlemen of the Committee, &c.* when there was no

Knight but himself." The occasion gives Cleveland a chance to
comment on the monstrosity of a singular man who conceives himself plural, when it may be that the genuine monstrosity that attracted Cleveland's attention was that of the sequestration ordinance itself.

The poem begins with the shouting of one who has uncovered a
freak suitable for a sideshow, and much of the raffishness of the
opening lines may well derive from the language of the barker:

> Hand out a flag, and gather pence! A piece
> Which *Africke* never bred, nor swelling *Greece*
> With stories timpany, a beast so rare
> No *Lecturers* wrought cap, nor *Bartlemew* Fare
> Can match him; Natures whimsey, one that out-vyes
> *Tredeskin* and his ark of Novelties.
>
> (1–6)

The wrought-cap we recognize from *"Square-Cap"* as a reference to
a Puritan, and Bartholomew Fair is such a place as suits the likes of a
monster. Tradescant's museum, or ark, was a collection of oddities
and wonders which later became the basis of the collection of the
Ashmolean Museum at Oxford. The tone of the poem is that of the
high-spirited discourse which recalls Donne and the energy of direct address he often developed in his songs. Some of the same
bemused irony shows up in these opening lines.

Cleveland makes a great deal out of the potential for monstrosity
which lies in the image of Martin's being more than what he is, and
we will see in the Smectymnuus poem that something of a remarkable resource is being tapped here—that Cleveland is at home talking about the monstrous. His poems on hermaphrodites are surely
in this vein; and his examination of the twinness present in human
anatomy in "Upon an Hermophrodite" is a clear preparation for the
attack on Martin, who is not merely "Natures whimsey," but "the
Gog and *Magog* of prodigious sights" (7). He even becomes plural in
his own right in a name which may have been applied to him regularly: "Sir *Thomas Knights.*" Once this plurality is established,
Cleveland specuates in mock innocence, "Are you Sir Thomas and
Sir *Martin* too?" (10). Then he proceeds to liken him to Issachar, the
biblical ass which bore a double burden: *"Issachar Couchant* 'twixt a
brace of Sirs" (11), but we see, too, that there is more than likeness

being played on here. The poem's controlling metaphor becomes what K. K. Ruthven calls an heraldic conceit.[6]

Cleveland makes an effort at a mock-description of the coat-of-arms of "Sir *Thomas Knights*"; and, though much of the humor is lost to modern eyes, his own audience would instantly have seen just how comical his results are. The line just quoted, with "*Issachar Couchant*," is a madcap assertion that Sir Thomas's arms bear an ass upon them, instead of, perhaps, a lion, which would more normally be "couchant." Such an assertion would have been witheringly comic in Cleveland's day, but even more witty is the reference to the ass being "*Couchant*," a perfectly obvious heraldic term meaning lying down with the head erect, since the biblical text itself is only mildly altered to yield the witty insight: "Issachar is a strong ass couching down between two burdens" (Genesis xlix. 14.).

Then, since either the spurs or the sword is the nominal sign of the knight, Cleveland chooses the spurs because they begin as one thing and branch out into two: "Spurs representative! thou that are able / To be a *Voider* to King *Arthurs* Table" (15–16), which demeans the allusion to knighthood by suggesting that Sir Thomas is suited to removing (voiding) the dirty dishes from Arthur's table. "Void" is also a term of heraldry meaning, ultimately, to make two parts, or couple-closes, of a single chevron or bar as it would appear on a shield, thus avoiding the chevron and permitting some of the field-color of the shield to show through. The heraldic issue develops until Cleveland has what he calls "this blazond Solecisme" (31) which "unites / Single soled Thomas to a yoake of Knights" (31–32). The blazon, a verbal description of a coat-of-arms, usually follows a carefully prescribed order, one that takes into account such aspects as the field and the heraldic objects on it. Actually, Cleveland is loose in his treatment of the blazon; he prefers humor to any kind of thoroughgoing accuracy, but he manages to use those portions of the blazon that amuse him.

The field, for instance, is described as being in extraordinary bad taste in the following lines: "But can a Knighthood on a Knighthood lie? / Mettal on Mettal is ill Armorie" (23–24). The reference to metal on metal means simply that gold or silver color is overlaid in the chevron or banner on the shield, and either the chevron or the banner is gold or silver. Usually the shield was either colored, half-colored, or metal, with a contrasting-color chevron or bar across it so the coat would be plainly identifiable from a distance in battle.

The metal on metal combination is like white on white; it cannot be readily identified and is, hence, "ill Armorie." Then there is the bifurcation implicit in the two metals on one and in the celebrated dualism of Sir Thomas himself. On this field, as already indicated, is the charge of the ass couchant; but Cleveland does not supply us with many more specific terms of the blazon: he does not have to.

One other bit of amusement is the comparison of Sir Thomas with Godfrey of Boulogne, since Godfrey's shield bore a figure that was metal on metal: five golden crosses on a field of silver. This comparison is a mockery since, apart from the papist associations Godfrey would have had and the fact that he died while on crusade, there is no reason to suspect that the comparison is anything but invidious. The same thing seems to be true of the following comparison with Julius Caesar, an even more ridiculous epic inflation. Cleveland recalls, from Suetonius, that Caesar at one time possessed two consulships because one, properly held by a man named Bibulus, was abandoned, for all practical purposes, to Caesar's operation. A less comparative and amusing point is made in suggesting that it is pedantic to preserve strict grammar (Priscian was an eminent grammarian and "*Priscan* bleeds with honour" means that grammar is imprecise). The point is that Sir Thomas's offense against grammar was that he did not keep his number in order.

The final couplet of the poem preserves a measure of ambiguity: "But is no matter, for *Amphibious* he / May have a Knight hang'd, yet Sir *Tom* go free." Thus, this Sir Tom can "hang" a knight, a genuine Royalist knight, while himself going free. Or, the lines can mean that, since there are two of him, one can hang while the other escapes. But this ambiguity is not stinging; it is not like the badger-bite of the keen iambics with which Cleveland draws blood later. The poem, with its progress from monstrosity to mere amphibiousness, is not ultimately as damaging as it is amusing.

III   *The Adulteries of Twisted Nature*

A much more vicious and uncompromising poem, one likely to be more appealing to the threatened Royalists and which contains the analysis of "all th' Adulteries of twisted nature" (33), is "*The Mixt Assembly,*" Cleveland's deliberately scurrilous attack on the Westminster Assembly. The attack, almost one hundred lines long, is brilliantly couched in biblical imagery; and Cleveland describes the chief persons of the Assembly—which ultimately agreed on the forms of worship for the new Parliamentary government—in terms which emphasized their hypocrisy. Cleveland's principal weapon is ridicule, but he achieves much of his effect by demonstrating his familiarity with the people prominent in the Assembly. However, the poem is not a mere character in the traditional mode, but rather a group portrait which in its ugliness and awful distortion recalls the later, carbuncular portraits of William Hogarth. Cleveland's is however, one of the most bestial and scatological attacks in the language—short of Jonathan Swift.

The Westminster Assembly was a collection of carefully chosen English divines, members of both Houses of Parliament, with a group of eight Scottish commissioners, totaling in all almost one hundred-forty members. A mixed assembly, it first met in July, 1643, though its formulation as a body was contemplated as early as 1641. The original impulse for creating and convening the assembly was drawn from Scottish insistence that the only solution for the religious difficulties brought upon them by Archbishop Laud and the resultant two Bishops' Wars was to make religious practice in England and Scotland uniform in nature. Ironically, this is exactly what Laud had in mind; but the Scots wanted not uniform Episcopacy but uniform Presbyterianism.

At first, Parliament was not terribly interested in such a proposal. Naturally it showed enough formal interest to keep the Scots from pressing further, but it held off making any specific recommendations for as long as it could. And, as long as it felt it could hold out in the field against the king, Parliament was not inclined to humor the Scots. However, after the military reversals in 1642, Parliament understood it could not do without Scottish military assistance; and the primary reward that the Scots could expect from their own involvement was the hope of a uniform mode of government and worship in the two kingdoms. The Solemn League and Covenant, including the Scottish, the English, and the Irish Covenanters, was agreed upon, which swore to uphold the Scottish church and to reform the English and Irish churches to conform with its tenets. This was a commitment, then, to make the churches of the three kingdoms presbyterian in form, to replace bishops with elders, the Book of Common Prayer with the *Directory* of worship, and to replace the king as head of the church with Parliament.

Things were never quite so simple as they might have been. The Independents and Puritans were most reluctant to accept Pres-

byterianism as it was practiced in Scotland. But military circumstances made it imperative, since the Scots had stopped the
king's forces twice before the Civil War; and, if the Scots were
somehow induced to join on the side of Charles, their kinsman, all
would be lost and parliamentary heads would roll. Consequently,
Parliament swallowed its objections and presented a "united front"[7]
to ensure victory. But Parliament privately expressed considerable
uncertainty. Particularly was this true of the Independents and sectaries, who viewed Scottish Presbyterianism as something short of
a genuine reform of church government.

The New Model Army under Cromwell was itself opposed to
instituting Presbyterianism in England since most of the New
Model were themselves Independents, or sectaries, who were
fighting to protect their own modes of worship. So ultimately the
union of Presbyter and Independent was very uneasy; the Presbyterians refused the easy toleration demanded by the Independents;
and the Independents yielded only after struggle and modification
to the demands that elders be elected throughout England. Finally,
the order for election was given; but, with more delays characteriz-
ing the entire proceedings, the number of elders actually settled
upon was small. We can see why Milton and Cleveland were both
dissatisfied with the developments of the assembly.

Much of this difficulty was unknown to Cleveland. He could not
have fully appreciated the struggles of the forces which sat in the
assembly, though he was fully capable of seeing what the results of
the assembly were likely to be. Consequently, he opens his attack
by citing the motley character of the group:

> Fleabitten Synod: an Assembly brew'd
> Of Clerks and Elders *ana*, like the rude
> Chaos of Presbyt'ry, where Lay-men guide
> With the tame Woolpack Clergie by their side.
> Who askt the Banes 'twixt these discolor'd Mates?
> A strange *Grottesco* this, the Church and States
> (Most divine tick-tack) in a pye-bald crew,
> To serve as table-men of divers hue.
>
>   (1–8)

The lines themselves are a mastery of confusion. "Synod" suggests
the worst associations of the papist councils to reform the church;
"Fleabitten" suggests the spotted coat of a bay or sorrel horse;

"tame Woolpack Clergie" is an attack on the perversion of a clergy that does not shepherd but is itself shepherded. All these rich and diverse suggestions pull simultaneously in many directions; for the Greek word *ana* is a pharmacist's term for the mixing of equal parts, here "Clerks and Elders," and the idea of mixing is reinforced by the term "brew'd," which finally rhymes with "rude/Chaos," which in turn reveals the nature of the mixture. But the assembly is more than a mere brew or concoction; therefore, line five, which questions the "Banes" (banns) announced for the "discolour'd Mates," declares the arrangement to be a veritable marriage. This metaphor is merely opprobrious until we see how deftly it is developed later when Cleveland gives thought to the "Adulteries of twisted nature." Only then do we see the metaphor's scabrous potential.

The metaphor which the first lines develop, that of the assembly as a concoction or prescription to be taken for an illness, is not abandoned after the opening of the poem. Such lines as "The Scepter and the Crosier are the Crutches, / Which if not trusted in their pious Clutches, / Will faile the Criple State" (25–28) and the reference to the feverish nightmares of the ill in "Be sick and dream a little, you may then / Phansie these Linsie-Woolsie Vestry-men" (51–52) show that the metaphor is not superficial. The state is ill; these men are both fashioning the medicine it will take and are at the same time the prescription itself. Cleveland makes it obvious that the medicine is worse than the sickness and could hardly be expected to accomplish a cure.

The poem continues in such a general vein, being only mildly specific until line fifty-three (the poem has ninety-eight lines), when the mode of address shifts rather abruptly. The tone of wry amusement which characterizes such a general attack as in the following lines gives way entirely to a mode which names names and scalds individual reputations:

> Strange Scarlet Doctors these, they'l passe in Story
> For sinners halfe refin'd in Purgatory;
> Or parboyl'd Lobsters, where there joyntly rules
> The fading Sables and the coming Gules.

> (37–40)

The last forty lines of the poem are among the most vicious lines Cleveland wrote, though what they are to become is only generally suggested by

> Forebeare good *Pembroke*, be not over-daring,
> Such Company may chance to spoile thy swearing;
> And these Drum-Major oaths of Bulke unruly,
> May dwindle to a feeble *By my truly*.
> Hee that Noble *Percyes* blood inherits,
> Will he strike up a *Hotspur* of the spirits?
> Hee'l fright the *Obadiahs* out of tune,
> With his uncircumcised *Algernoon*.
>
> (53–60)

Both these men are peculiar for their having been aristocrats of the same quality as most of the cavaliers. And though Pembroke was long an ardent Presbyterian, *"Algernoon"* was of the same blood as "the Noble *Percyes*" and had once commanded the king's fleet. It has been said that Percy's act of turning the fleet over to Parliament was one of the most damaging blows to King Charles in the course of the war. Cleveland's treatment of both these figures is curious: he had no reason to have the historian's perspective in regard to Percy, and he could hardly hold him responsible for having significantly undone the king. But unless Percy's quality recommended him even beyond his deeds (a not unlikely possibility), such deferential treatment seems unusually respectful.

The most important benefit Pembroke and Percy derive from such treatment is their exclusion from taking part in the "dance of the Westminster Assemblymen,"[8] an obscene parody of the court dances which represented platonic order, harmony, and divine union in the happier times when the court would have been the gathering place for many of these men. Cleveland was well prepared for this moment in the poem, having had considerable poetic experience in developing and describing dances and the pairing-off they usually entail. Few metaphors could have more adequately expressed the dark perversion of the mixture of men at this assembly, particularly when one reflects on the general nature of the dance in normal circumstances. An obvious irony exists in having them all dancing a Scottish dance:

> A Jig, a Jig: And in this Antick dance
> *Fielding* and doxy *Marshall* first advance.
> *Twiss* blowes the Scotch pipes, and the loving brase
> Puts on the traces, and treads Cinqu-a-pace.
> Then *Say and Seale* must his old Hamstrings supple,

And he and rumpl'd *Palmer* make a couple.
Palmer's a fruitfull girle, if hee'l unfold her,
The Midwife may finde worke about her shoulder.
Kimbolton, that rebellious *Boanerges*,
Must be content to saddle Doctor *Burges*.
If *Burges* get a clap, 'tis ne're the worse,
But the fift time of his Compurgators.

(67–78)

The dance is ultimately a variety of the antimasque in the tradition of the dance of Comus and his crew, Bacchus and his pards, and of Circe and her swine. Cleveland makes horses of his men, gives them clap, suggests scurrilous sexual relations of a sodomic order, and he investigates, ultimately, not merely the sexual acts implied in the lines but the outcome of those acts:

Pym and the *Members* must their giblets levy
T' incounter Madam *Smec*, that single Bevy.
If they two truck together, 'twill not be
A Childbirth, but a Gaole-Deliverie.

(83–86)

The grotesque vision which all these lines produce is worthy of the next age, but it is also one of the most natural of visions for Cleveland, who had a gift for divining the monstrous (or making monstrous the divine).

The only member of the assembly Cleveland spares is the great scholar John Selden," the walking library." Selden is not excused from dancing, but he does not dance a jig and he does not have a partner: "hee's a Galliard by himself . . . there's more Divines in him / Then in all this their Jewish *Sanhedrim*" (88–90). But he is the only exception. Twisse is finally accused of permitting "the Ox and Asse go yok'd in the same plough" (94), thus breaking Moses' law as expressed in Deuteronomy xii. 10. Twisse is chided as a mere incompetent in Cleveland's comparison of him with Lord Brooke's preacher, said to have been a common coachman possessed, like John Bunyan, with the gift of preaching. John Spencer, the coachman-preacher, would never have gotten his animals so confused.

Looking back at the beginning of the poem, we see that the "Fleabitten synod," in the opening line, is no casual reference. The metamorphosis from English divine to jogging nag and jigging "hagg" (65) has begun in the very first line and continues to the end of the poem. And we realize that the poem is virtually a bestiary, with a most remarkable inventory of animals of land, sea, and air. We have mentioned the constant reference to horses and sheep, the allusion to Isaachar, the ox and the ass, and the "parboyl'd Lobsters." But there is also a reference to "the flea that *Falstaffe* damn'd"[9] (41), as well as one to "*Royston* Crowes, who are (as I may say) / Friers of both the Orders *Black* and *Gray*" (19–20).

Finally, and as a way of epitomizing the mixed circumstances he memorializes here, Cleveland says, "Oh that they were in chalk and charcole drawn! / The Misselany Satyr, and the Fawne" (31–32), who, as half-god, half-beast, represent not only the ultimate in confusion and admixture, but the darker forces of sexual license and perversion which operate metaphorically later in the poem. "The Mixt Assembly" is indeed a strange pastoral poem. Its subject is pastors; its metaphor is a dance; its allusions are both classical and modern; its potential for redeeming pastoral innocence (and sin) is implied in the Christian circumstances of the genuine assembly. But all the potential to goodness is lost through perversion. Not even John Selden can rescue, in the traditional heroic manner, his men from Circe's charms. The synod is fleabitten at first and fleabitten at last.

IV   *Smectymnuus: Marriage and Monstrosity*

The metaphors of marriage and monstrosity found an easy application in "Smectymnuus, *or the Club-Divines,*" a treatment of a theme Cleveland refers to in other poems: the Smectymnuus controversy. This poem, ninety-eight lines long, is in essence an attempt at "definition" of the word, "Smectymnuus." It treats the word etymologically, anatomically (by breaking down its parts), and genealogically in a vain effort to understand it. The entire poem sounds reminiscent of the kinds of undergraduate prolusions Cleveland would have written at Christ's College. All the invention he can bring to bear will not unravel the knot, and neither will it yield intelligibility and sense.

Smectymnuus gives Cleveland a chance to get all his "hee-goats" milked, though he spurns Smectymnuus in a number of poems early-on; and, whenever he gets the chance to attack the "monster," he does so. The name "Smectymnuus" comes from the conjunction

of the first letters of the names of five divines who wrote and published a tract in March, 1641, about the merits of bishop and presbyter, whether they are equal or unequal. The men were, in the order
in which their names were used for the pseudonym, Stephen Mar-
shall, Edmund Calamy, Thomas Young, Matthew Newcomen, and
William Spurstow. Their tract was a reply to Bishop Hall's *A Humble Remonstrance*, published in 1640; and after their tract was published Bishop Hall attacked them in turn. Milton himself came to
the aid of the Smectymnuuns (Young had been his tutor) in the
attack on Hall.

But what interests Cleveland is not the contents of the Smectym-
nuun's tract, though Cleveland was concerned insofar as it attacked
the establishment of bishops. The phenomenon of Smectymnuus
itself is the attraction, just as in his poem on "Sir Thomas Knights";
and issues at stake take a role subordinate to the possibilities of wit.
Cleveland, like many of the cavaliers, is amused by the outrageous
name of the "author" of the tract; therefore, he centers his attack on
this factor in such lines as "Five faces lurke under one single viz-
zard" (32), though he develops a slightly different line of imagery in:

> The Banes are askt, would but the times give way,
> Betwixt *Smectymnuus* and *Et caetera*.
> The Guests invited by a friendly Summons,
> Should be the Convocation and the Commons.
> The Priest to tie the Foxes tailes together,
> *Moseley*, or *Sancta Clara*, chuse you whether,
> See, what an off-spring every one expects!
> What strange Plurality of Men and Sects!
>
> (75–82)

Thus, in marrying documents from both sides of the struggle,
Cleveland gives expression to his genuine confusion at the zeal and
ardentry of religious controversialists of the day. The last line of the
passage quoted is not mock wonderment; Cleveland is honestly
amazed at the excitement such minor issues can arouse in the minds
of others. And it is partly because such excitement is not likely to
take hold of him that he can write with the peculiar detachment that
characterizes so much of his poetry. He is not attracted to the
substance of the Smectymnuus tracts simply because the problems
of choosing between bishop and presbyter do not strike him as
serious—at least not as religious problems. He is well aware of the

seriousness of the implications for a political system; but when writing this poem, such seriousness did not seem important enough to develop. To have taken the controversy seriously would have been to grace it with undue importance: such was not Cleveland's purpose. His purpose was ridicule, pure and simple; and he begins by ridiculing the name:

> *Smectymnuus?* The Goblin makes me start:
> I' th' Name of Rabbi *Abraham,* what art?
> *Syriac?* or *Arabick?* or *Welsh?* what skilt?
> Ap all the Bricklayers that *Babell* built.
> Some Conjurer translate, and let me know it:
> Till then 'tis fit for a West-Saxon Poet.
>
> (1–6)

He postures as a questioner, mock-ignorant, asking whether the word be Hebrew, Syriac, or something else, concluding ultimately that it is polyglot. He then heaps the normal obloquy upon it which is implied in connecting it with Babel and the barbarisms (as his time understood them) of primitive English poetry. None of these barbs are terribly stinging, but then Cleveland does not consider the subject worthy of the badger-bite he develops for more serious affairs. His own image in the poem adequately describes the power of his barrage: "Which like a Porcupine presents a Muster, / And shoots his quills at Bishops and their Sees" (12–13).

"Smectymnuus" is essentially a poem which treats a subject according to the rules of invention which we have already seen at work in earlier poems. Cleveland adopts a stance or proposes a comparison and then exhausts his store of comparatives in an effort to ridicule the Smectymnuuns while treating his audience to the richness of his wit. The first lines propose the possibility that "Smectymnuus" is a foreign word, and the images which fill out the beginnings of the poem dwell on that possibility, using comparatives which have themselves pejorative connotations.

Once that point has been made, Cleveland admits that the word is a name which represents a "Brother-hood" which may intend to "Out-brave us with a name in Rank and File, / A Name which if 'twere train'd would spread a mile" (9–10). That last line is itself a wittily lengthy line to accommodate the sense; but examination shows that, though it looms physically longer than the lines before and after it, it has a normal ten syllables and that the effect of length is achieved by the choice of words. And, after calling the brother-hood a "devout litter of young *Maccabees*" (14), Cleveland compares them with *"Don Quixots* Rosary of Slaves / Strung on a chaine" (19–20), with a "Murnivall of Knaves" (four Jacks in one hand in the card-game Gleek), and then with Gypsies. He finally nullifies their satirical bite by metaphorically drawing their teeth: "So the vaine Satyrists stand in a row, / As hollow teeth upon a Lute-string show" (23–24).

The monstrosity of the "Brother-hood" is the subject of the fol-lowing comparison with a modern monster:

> Th' *Italian* Monster pregnant with his Brother,
> Natures *Dyaeresis*, halfe one another,
> He, with his little Sides-man *Lazarus*,
> Must both give way unto *Smectymnuus*.
> Next *Sturbridge-Faire* is *Smec's*; for loe his side
> Into a five fold *Lazar's* multipli'd.
>
> (25–30)

The reference is to a Genoese, Lazarus Colloredo, who was re-ported to have had a small brother growing out of his side.[10] The implication, naturally, is that "Smec" would becloud even the odd-est freaks at the most celebrated of English fairs. Then follows (33–48) a catalog of undeveloped comparisons with a wide variety of compoundings—from the notion that "Smec" is a challenge for Pythagoras's vision of the transmigration of souls (the soul would have to stop at fivefold "Smec"), through the "Scotch Marke" which "shrinkes to thirteen pence," on to "the Decalogue in a single pen-ny." And, in the cases of these latter compoundings, the problem of monstrosity is lost sight of: all that remains is the notion of numer-ous things contained in one.

The bulk of the poem thereafter is a recitation, virtually breath-less at that, of as many allusions to amusing conjunctions as Cleve-land can invent. His sources are biblical ("the *Sadduces* would raise a question, / Who must be *Smec* at th' Resurrection" [53–54]), clas-sical, and modern; Cleveland shows slight concern about how the three are mixed together. A rather typical passage, which draws comparisons from a remarkably diverse group of sources, is this verse paragraph:

> *Caligula,* whose pride was Mankinds Baile,
> As who disdain'd to murder by retaile,
> Wishing the world has but one generall Neck,
> His glutton blade might have found game in *Smec.*
> No Eccho can improve the Authour more,
> Whose lungs pay use on use to halfe a score.
> No Fellon is more letter'd, though the brand
> Both superscribes his shoulder and his hand.
> Some Welch-man was his Godfather; for he
> Weares in his name his Genealogie.
>
> (65–74)

Such lines have the satirical roughness that Cleveland recommended in his poem on Guy Fawkes, but the roughness does not
seem to emanate only from "Classhing tearms" or even from "Indignation"; it derives from the diversity of comparisons lumped
together, each developed hardly further than a couplet. There is
none of the outrage or the "firy passion" which concerned Cleveland
in "On the Pouder Plot"; instead, the effect of coarseness is worked
up from the arbitrariness of the four comparisons which begin with
Rome and end with Wales. Such a confusion is itself whimsical to a
significant degree; and, were it not for the fact that "Smec" more
amuses Cleveland than threatens him, such whimsy would scuttle
the poem entirely. As it is, the poem suffers from too great a length
(ninety-eight lines) and from a too-low level of intensity—
particularly in view of the limited excitement of the wit in most
passages. Only rarely does the poem breath any life, and its opening
is the most lively and interesting section.

A striking comparison can be made between this poem and the
refined and elegantly developed *"Upon the Kings return from Scotland."* The comparison is particularly useful because the poems
were written close to one another in time, if not in mood. They were
written some time shortly before the end of 1641, with the king's
return probably having been celebrated first. The immediate
suggestion that derives from such a comparison is the possibility
that the poem on "Smec" may be as rough as it is strictly in an effort
to answer to the needs of satire, since the poem on the king's return,
while clearly very witty, and most enlightened in its amusement, is
by no means bitingly satirical. However, both poems open with
much the same kind of rhetorical stance of direct address, and "The
Kings Return" develops the same kind of structure: the poet cites

comparisons with the king's motion which are witty in that they all imply countermotion. The difference is in the absence of unusual roughness in "The King's Return," and in the fact that this poem is less than half the length of the poem on "Smec."

V "The King's Return": Invention and Hope

"The King's Return" was published first in a university miscellany, *Irenodia Cantabrigiensis* (1641), and was not published in the first collected edition of 1647, nor in any edition until 1659. In forty-two elegant, complimentary lines, Cleveland tries to iron out the difficulties inherent in the king's visit to Scotland, a visit which had serious implications for the future of Charles I's government. Essentially, Cleveland is excusing the visit by means of elaborate rhetorical invention and wit-play. At first he refuses to believe the king has left at all, but he finally agrees that if he did go he went "by a double motion," and his return is like a "Counterpane" to warm the South.

The poem shows none of the irascibility that characterizes the satires, which by comparison seem almost unstudied. We observe how the first lines echo the beginning of "Smec," but how they resolve themselves into the characteristic polysyllabic effect in the final word, "Zodiack":

> Return'd? I'll ne'r believe't; First prove him hence;
> Kings travel by their beams and influence.
> Who says the soul gives out her gests, or goes
> A flitting progresse 'twixt the head and toes?
> She rules by Omnipresence, and shall we
> Denie a Prince the same ubiquitie?
> Or grant he went, and 'cause the knot was slack,
> Girt both the nations with his Zodiack.
>
> (1–8)

It is no accident that some of the same imagistic energy Cleveland later used in "The Kings Disguise" should be developed here. The king is more like a spirit than a mere man, he is likened to the sun itself traveling on "beams and influence," and he is characterized by omnipresence. The prince can not be denied the privileges of the soul and spirit; and, if it be granted he left the nation at all, it must also be granted he left in order to prove more conclusively the power of his influence (zodiac) and to embrace the Scottish nation closer to him. The opening of the poem is a characteristic rhetorical disclaimer of that which is obviously true, along with the normal addition of a tag to explain the true meaning of what must be granted.

But the images of sun and spirit do not totally dominate the poem; what dominates it is the essential contradiction of countermotion. The grounds for the denial of motion, which the first several lines represent, are found in the image of the recoil: all motion forward imples motion backward. Thus all such action bears with it its own denial: "Hither and hence at once; thus every sphere / Doth by a double motion enter-fere" (13–14). Cleveland realizes how much of a logical ploy such reasoning is; how it falls short of being true; and how, particularly, it falls short of convincing us that Charles both went and stayed, even though it may be true that a tree grows downward in its roots, just as it grows upward in its shoots (9–10). Cleveland's logical position is much the same as it has been in other poems: to convince us by a plenitude of examples rather than by showing us exactly how this subject is likened to his examples. Handbooks of logic of the day talk about a "band" which binds a subject to what it is being compared with; and the "band" in this poem, as in many others, is never truly expressed, but merely implied.

The force of comparisons such as "Backward is forward in the Hebrew tongue" (34), a favorite of Cleveland's, is supposed to be self-evident and axiomatic, a "proof" that the king can seem to be going in one direction while actually going in the other: "his feet still contradict him as he goes" (24). Thus it is enough to weight the argument with such statements as "the bullet flying makes the gun recoyl" (26) and "Islands go back but when you're under sail" (32). But one of the most awful and most prophetic of images is near the end of the poem—the mixing of blood and milk, with all its implications of life and death (already treated explicitly in lines 27–30): "Now the Church-militant in plentie rests, / Nor fears like th' Amazon to lose her breasts. / Her means are safe, not squees'd untill the blood / Mix with the milk and choke the tender brood" (35–38).

In this image Cleveland gets to some of the fearsome and disturbing aspects of the king's journey; we begin to understand that the apparent confidence Cleveland has in the king is not pure and not total. Saintsbury accused this poem of being "weak and pithless," but he may not have felt Cleveland was expressing doubt along with his celebratory university confidence. The facts of the king's visit, some of which were known to Cleveland and to most Englishmen, indicate that he had a great deal to answer for at home. His "motions" were indeed curious and not susceptible to prediction: only the historian, with an understanding of Charles's constant efforts to make a "deal" at almost any cost with his opponents, including that of offering up his most trusted advisors to the block, would have been able to make sense of his behavior. A faithful servant like Cleveland, fresh from the execution of Strafford in May, could only have been bewildered by the king's actions in this his first "flight" to the Scotch.

Ostensibly, King Charles went to Scotland to ensure unity with that kingdom and to relieve the pressure of the standing Scots army which had defeated his own forces in the Bishop's Wars. Actually, he went to see if he could count on the Scots to aid him in his struggle with Parliament. To that end, he acquiesced to a surprising number of formal shows of accepting Scottish demands. He not only listened to Scotland's most important preachers, but took part enthusiastically in Presbyterian services himself, finally ratifying into law the acts of the Scottish parliament which established Presbyterianism as the official religion of Scotland.[11] The chances are that Charles might have made considerable progress with the Scots if it had not been for the uncovering of a plot against the life of Argyll, a prominent Scottish leader. The "incident" ended all negotiations, and an enraged English Parliament was glad to see Charles return empty-handed—just as, for different reasons, were many Royalists.

How much of the relatively secret purposes of King Charles's mission was known to Cleveland is difficult to say. The king's cooperation with the outward forms of Scottish religion must have been known in both kingdoms almost immediately. Parliament was aware of its own difficulties with Charles and must not have been hard put to sense many of his motives. Obviously, if Charles could placate the Scots—despite Laud's efforts at uniformity—and win them to his side, Parliament would be virtually powerless to force Charles to accept its views. But how completely Scotland held the key to the future of the struggle between Charles and Parliament no one could have said at that time. Cleveland's contempt for the Scots was yet to be given vent. We see some of it in his splenetic rage over the affairs of the Westminster Assembly, but, of course, the most lasting poem he wrote on the subject was yet to come. Even a poet known to be as prophetic as Cleveland could only hope to sense uncertainty about Scottish relations at the time of writing his contribution to the miscellany.

Nevertheless, Cleveland would have had innumerable misgivings about Charles's behavior. For one thing, he could hardly have been overjoyed at the prospect of Charles's sitting placidly before Scottish preachers who were promulgating a religion which only months before Charles had virtually agreed to help exterminate. The thought that Presbyterianism might one day be the authorized religion of both kingdoms was doubtless far from the mind of anyone involved in any of the three contentious parties, though, as it turned out, such a thought would have been most repugnant to those who were to become defined as Royalists and loyal to the king. That the king should give signs of not being loyal to himself was rather frightening, and Cleveland's treatment of the subject offers every evidence of his willingness to "invent" for his sovereign and argue a case for him which shows his causes to be just causes.

Cleveland's willingness to invent leads to a point of first importance about the poem and its strategy. In effect, the poem gives indications of its being structured somewhat on the lines of an oration, not only by virtue of its being essentially a poem delivered in direct address, but also by virtue of its efforts to prove a case by means of marshalling conclusive examples which argue by themselves, by precedent. Such poetry is common in the seventeenth century, and the use of legal language and a legal approach should hardly be surprising from a poet who was himself at the Law Line. Likewise, the form of the legal, or forensic, oration, one of the three accepted forms for the oration, should be one of the most natural modes for a law student who was once also Rhetoric Reader for the university.

The entire poem is an effort to acquit Charles of the charge of having gone to Scotland for any but the most natural reasons, and Cleveland's strategy is to put the burden of proof on his imaginary opponent: "First prove him hence." Then, granting his opponent the point that perhaps Charles had indeed gone, he takes the sting out of it entirely by showing how being gone implies nothing other than returning—or not having left in fact at all. The examples and arguments he cites account for the bulk of the poem; and, when he has done with them, he declares Charles to be acquitted. He uses two legal terms in the process, the second of which accents nothing other than the fact that Charles and his subjects are counterparts ("Counterpane" reads "counterpart" in Saintsbury, and means "counterpart of an indenture"): "Quits Charles; Our souls did guard him northward thus, / Now He the Counterpane comes South to us." It is not so difficult to see why Charles was not so soon "Quits" in "The King's Disguise," even though there, too, Cleveland's hopes were similarly expressed in such lines as: "May thy strange journey contradictions twist, / And force faire weather from a Scottish mist" ("The Kings Disguise," 117–118). The contradictions twisted in both these journeys were more impossible to unwind than John Cleveland would ever have imagined, given his unyielding faithfulness to Charles and to his cause. But the painfulness of his poems on the subjects reveal a good deal about Cleveland's own unsettled state of mind: his arguments were as much with himself as with an imaginary opponent.

VI *Keen Iambicks and the Rebell Scot*

But there was no thought of argument when Cleveland came to writing *"The Rebell* Scot," the most famous and successful of all his poems, and the most thoroughgoing attack on the Scots any English poet had ever written. The pressure for such an attack had been building steadily, as we can see from Cleveland's reactions to the events of the day, which seemed to grow more and more involved with Scottish interests. What triggered this final giving away to almost total rage was what was indeed to prove the last and final stroke: the Scottish intervention on the side of Parliament.

Charles had undertaken the siege of Gloucester in August and September, 1643, a siege which, for the sake of morale and strategy, should have been successful. Charles's original plans of attacking London with a three-part army had to be abandoned partly because of the failure of his armies to cleave together and agree to his plans. Gloucester was then a kind of consolation for being unable to carry out the original plan. And when Charles besieged the town his own cause was, despite the loss of London, probably never stronger. Winning at Gloucester could very well have helped keep the Scots out of the war, but even having been soundly defeated would have perhaps kept the Scots in Scotland. But Charles simply could not make the siege work, and he had to retreat when Essex and a reinforcing Parliamentary army moved toward him. The uncertainty of the situation was such that Pym, the most influential man in Parliament, finally decided to take steps with his plans for an alliance, plans that resulted in "The Solemn League and Covenant" and that bound England to Scotland not only politically but religiously. Scotland had long been arguing for such an alliance; but, had King Charles been victorious in the field, it might not have been quite so anxious to join forces with Parliament. As it was, Scotland represented the balance of power and was correct in its assumptions about the strength of Charles's forces.

Pym died in December, 1643, of a mysterious disease, described by some as an internal abscess, which apparently rendered him virtually impossible to be near. If, as the suggestion seems to be, he developed some kind of overpowering stench, it must have been extraordinary to have been perceived by the people of that time, since they were daily victim to odors we would find unimaginable. The Scots crossed the border in January, 1644, and thus Pym never lived to see the results of the agreements he had engineered. The results were considerable and were felt almost immediately. The Parliamentary forces, with the aid of the Scots, gained total control of the north countries after the battle of Marston Moor, which Prince Rupert lost partly because he sustained an attack after his armies had broken rank for the night. Charles suffered several more defeats even before Cromwell's New Model Army was formed and swept the field.

But Cleveland's rage is aimed at the fact of rebellion. Charles was a Scot and should have had allegiance from those of his own blood, and for Cleveland such a betrayal was like parricide: it represented a consummate and unforgivable evil. This betrayal for Cleveland is a monstrosity; and the opening lines of the poem concentrate on the unnatural and the monstrous qualities of Scottish invasion; and Cleveland's training as an observer of the monstrous is brought to full flower here:

> How? Providence? and yet a Scottish crew?
> Then Madam Nature wears black patches too:
> What? shall our Nation be in bondage thus
> Unto a Land that truckles under us?
> Ring the bells backward; I am all on fire,
> Not all the buckets in a Countrey Quire
> Shall quench my rage.

(1–7)

But the monstrous is more subtle here than in other poems which take inspiration from the sideshow freaks and harmless entertainments. Nature herself is deformed; the word of God is taken in vain by a Scottish crew ("Providence" was a war cry of the New Model Army); England is put in bondage to a nation whose natural position (like the bottom half of a trundle or "truckle" bed) is subservient to it; and the end of it all is that Cleveland is afire with rage, so much so that not all the water buckets of the average church choir (where the buckets were stored) could begin to quench it. He is talking not about that which is ugly and amusing, but that which is ugly and destructive—that which will consume and blast and ultimately destroy.

Yet his rage is such that not even it can suffice to keep him on the mark of his attack, nor can the explosives of Judas, Judge, or preacher (13–22) serve to treat a "Countrey sicke of *Pym's* disease" (10); he needs to be a magician as well:

> Yet to expresse a *Scot,* to play that prize,
> Not all those mouth-Granadoes can suffice.
> Before a *Scot* can properly be curst,
> I must (like *Hocus*) swallow daggers first.
>
> (23–26)

Of course, he swallows them only to disgorge them at their mark, relying on the magic "charm in verse" to preserve him, like an antidote, from the heat and fire of his own speech. And, when he has spent the first twenty-six lines of the poem getting his own posture clearly formed relative to his subject and to the writing of a proper curse, he talks about the traditional iambic attack of the satire. These lines are among the best known in the poem; and, while doubtless influenced by Horace and other classical poets, they ring with a peculiar personal tone:

> Come kéen *Iambicks,* ‖ with your Bádgers feét,
> And Bádgĕr-like, bite till your teéth dŏ meét.
> Help yĕ tárt Sátyrists, tŏ imp my ráge,
> With all the Scórpions thăt should whip this age.
> Scóts are líke Witchĕs; ‖ dŏ bŭt whét your pén,
> Scrátch til the blóod cóme; ‖ théy'l nŏt húrt yŏu thén.
> Nów as the Mártyrs were inforc'd tŏ táke

The shăpes ŏf beásts, like hýpŏcrĭtes, aᵗ stake,
I'lé báit mў Scót śo; ‖ yĕt nŏt chéat yoŭr eýes,
Ă Scót wĭthiń ă beást iš nó diśguĭse.

(27–36)

Among the interesting features of these lines is the meter and rhythm, their proper subject, as the first line tells us. An analysis, already indicated by marking of stress, shows that the lines which speak about iambics are not rhythmically iambic. Perhaps tormented by rage, they show clear signs of strain and displacement of accent, though there is a kind of decorum achieved by talking about iambics coming and then making them indeed come.

For instance, the first two lines might be treated metrically as hemistichs: the second five syllables of each follow the same pattern of anapest followed by iamb. But the first five syllables of each are varied. In the first line, a spondee is followed by an irregular foot while, in the second line, an amphimacer is followed by a spondee. The interesting thing about the lines is the use of three-syllable feet, a practice which is very curious for the age, and one which is even more curious for the age which is to come. The following line ends with iambs, just as the first two do; but the inversions are limited to the first two feet. The fourth line may be scanned as perfectly regular, but reading "that" as an unaccented syllable seems much preferable to giving it an artificial accent. The effect achieved is that of an accelerando beginning with the elision of "-ions" into one syllable, thus virtually imitating the idea of a whiplike motion. "Scots are like Witches; do but whet your pen" is a remarkable line in that it is perfectly symmetrical; it is broken in two five-syllable hemistichs which mirror each other: dactyl, trochee; anapest, iamb.

Such a virtuoso use of three-syllable feet and the exploration of dividing lines into two equal parts, searching for balance and antithesis of rhythms in the matching of the parts, is characteristic of the entire passage. Hardly a line of these is unworthy of close examination, but the value of the examination becomes quite plain when we come to the end of the lines and see that the next to last line is broken medially with a caesura, or pause, with halves of two feet each: probably meant to model the first line of the quotation exactly: spondee, irregular foot, anapest, iamb. A reasonable reading, of course, might accent "not," thus avoiding complete repetition. But, exact or not, the balance of three syllable feet and one syllable feet in that line is what "sets up" the last line and gives us the feeling of surprise, delight, and completion that we get from the witty line "A *Scot* within a beast is no disguise."

The effect is somewhat similar to those we have seen earlier, when Cleveland develops a technical or expressive polysyllable by way of contrast with plain speech. The fact that the last line finally gives us the regular iambics the first line promised long before, and the fact that this last line is truly "biting," should help us see that Cleveland's effects are not just "skin deep." He works closely and carefully beneath the immediately visible surface of the poem to make sure we feel the response he wants. When he invokes "keen iambicks," he does so perfectly consciously and with a willingness to invent the kind of metrical texture against which they will have real value.

The lengthy verse paragraph (fifty-eight lines) which follows explores some highly complex and witty circumstances relating to the idea of the Scots's being beasts, both in and out of disguise. The lines are difficult for anyone unfamiliar with a number of myths about the banishing long since of snakes from Ireland and wolves from England. The names of loyal Scots like Montrose and Crawford, if it is not known that these are examples of loyal and good Scotsmen as Cleveland sees them, are troublesome, just as are the references to London Tower and its commander, Sir William Balfour, who was dismissed by King Charles, but who turned up later as a commander of troops in the field against him.

We are on more generally familiar grounds in such lines as:

> Natŭre hĕr selfe dŏth Scótch-mĕn beásts cŏnfessĕ,
> Makĭng thĕir Coúntrĕy sŭch ă wíldĕrnessĕ:
> Ă Lánd thăt bríngs ĭn quéstiŏn ănd sŭspénse
> Gods ŏmnĭpresĕnce, ‖ bŭt thăt *Charles* cáme thénce:
> Bŭt thăt *Montrose* ănd *Crawfords* lóyăll Bánd
> Attón'd thĕir síns, ănd christ'nĕd halfe thĕ Lánd.
> Nŏr ĭs ĭt all thĕ Natĭŏn hăth thĕsĕ spóts;
> Thĕre ĭs ă Chúrch, ăs wéll ăs *Kirk* ŏf Scóts:
> Ăs ĭn ă píctŭre, whĕre thĕ squíntĭng páint̮
> Shĕwĕs Fiénd ŏn thĭs side, ănd ŏn thát side Saínt.

(47–56)

Therefore, except for the fact that Charles himself was a Scot and a product of an otherwise cursed land, there would be some doubt in the postulation of God's being present throughout His world.

Cleveland assures us that only the heroes who stood by Charles redeem the foulness of their nation, thereby putting Montrose and Crawford in the position of Christ redeemer or John the Baptist, an elevation to which they were not properly deserving, naturally. But what Cleveland is doing is condemning Scotland broadside while trying to be somewhat selective in his hits. He is not out to condemn the nation indiscriminately (but there are lines in the poem which show his readiness to do so), since Charles himself owes his birthright to the country; consequently, Cleveland's iambics must be keen, biting, and also extraordinarily cautious.

A metrical analysis of these lines suggests that Cleveland is not about to miss a chance to use rhythm effectively, as in the fourth line of the quotation; but he is by no means using rhythm as carefully as he does in lines in which meter is part of his proper subject. The most famous lines in the poem, which follow very closely, are iambic until the last when the pattern of the hemistich of "Come keen *Iambicks*" seems to be suggested again:

> Ă Land wherĕ onĕ maў praý with curst iñtent,
> Ŏ maý theў neveř suffeř banishment!   .
> Hăd *Cáin* beĕn *Scót*, Gód would have chang'd his doóme,
> Not forc'd him wandeř, ‖ but confin'd him home.

> (61–64)

These lines thrilled Dryden; he felt they were "wit in any language." Their effectiveness is by no means inconsiderable, particularly in view of the peculiar metrical qualities which are achieved by the use of the hemistich.

One thing that, perhaps, we should make clear is that the analysis we offer of the meter is always subject to question. It is quite possible to read these lines, which we describe as hemistichs with a single triple foot, as being normally iambic. However, when we do so, we disregard natural and meaningful accent; it is done in the name of regularity and metrical stress. Our analysis emphasizes meaning and rhythm rather than meter and enforced regularity. We also have in mind the fact that Cleveland has been referred to as the first poet in the language who used a conscious and sustained triple foot in his poems (in "A Song of Marke Antony"), a fact which makes it by no means impossible to think of Cleveland as offering a metrical twist of this subtlety.

Cleveland has not abandoned, of course, his more usual practice of securing a moment of wit by inserting a polysyllable at a crucial point, usually at the end of a couplet, as in the lines "They're Citizens o' the World; they're all in all, / Scotland's a Nation Epidemicall" (69–70). An analysis of the meter shows the return to iambs, and the wit of "Epidemicall" lies in its meaning and in its compression of half a line—five syllables—into one word. And the imagery of illness, derived from *"Pym's* disease," is developed in the predictably scatological and perverse detail of

> Sure *England* hath the Hemerods, and these
> On the North Posterne of the patient seize,
> Like Leeches: thus they physically thirst
> After our blood, but in the cure shall burst.
>
> (83–86)

Apart from its obviously vile character as an attack on the Scots, the imagery of hemorrhoids is rather daring since the the postern in question is Northern, not Southern. This underscores all the more the unnatural and parasitic quality of the leechlike Scots. And the leeches suggest, despite their overwhelming ugliness, something of the hopefulness of recovery for England. Cleveland may be grasping at straws, but it is nonetheless his hope.

Meanwhile, as an aid to hope, Cleveland recommends arms as the ready and immediate way of restoring the kingdoms to health: "'tis steel must tame / The stubborn *Scot:* A Prince that would reclaime / Rebells by yeelding, doth like him (or worse) / Who sadled his own back to shame his horse" (91–94). Steel, as well as shot, was being employed liberally at the time the poem was written; but it did no more good than yielding might have done. The last verse paragraph, some thirty lines, abandons the metaphor of illness and takes a most direct approach to chastising the Scots. Cleveland calls the Scots "proud Impostors" (111), "a race / Able to bring the Gibbet in disgrace" (114–15), and develops one of the last of his indirect metaphors: "The Indian that heaven did forsweare, / Because he heard the Spaniards were there, / Had he but knowne what Scots in hell had been, / He would *Erasmus*-like have hung between" (117–20).

The image of the Indian hanging "Erasmus-like" between heaven and hell is, to be sure, an odd one coming as it does at the end of the poem. The Indian has his savagery in common with the Scot, as Cleveland understands it, though the Indian may be somewhat ahead of the Scot by virtue of not sharing his religion. But, whatever commonalities may be seen between the two, the all-too-general quality of the image seems diffuse and relatively weak at a point which should be the strongest in the poem. One of the difficulties with the poem is that it drags itself to an end. Having worked up a healthy (early) attack, and having written some lasting lines, Cleveland let himself expatiate too broadly on his theme—perhaps because he fully understood he would have the rewards of an indulgent audience. But the modern audience is no longer quite so indulgent and no longer quite so quick to thrill to an attack on the savage Picts.

Consequently, the very last lines of the poem lose, for the modern reader, much of the focus and clarity which had been achieved earlier and seem strangely wasteful of energy which had built up to something of a remarkable pitch:

> My Muse hath done. A Voider for the nonce!
> I wrong the Devill, should I picke the bones.
> That dish is his: for when the Scots decease,
> Hell like their Nation feeds on Barnacles.
>   A Scot, when from the Gallow-Tree got loose,
>   Drops into *Styx*, and turnes a Soland-Goose.
>
>   (121–26)

The first phrase, "My Muse hath done," is immediately reminiscent of the style of the academic prolusion, which made full use of such rhetorical flourishes. The imagery of Cleveland as having picked his victim clean is clear enough, though it is not well integrated with the predominant imagery of the poem as a whole—not that that would bother a true enthusiast of Cleveland. But the modern reader loses contact with the poem with the references to barnacles and Soland geese, part of a legend which apparently had wide currency in Cleveland's day and earlier (see Morris and Withington's notes, with references to Browne and Butler).

The barnacles which fell from the trees in the Orkney Islands were said to drop in the water and turn into Soland geese; hence, Cleveland's wit-play is humorous though by no means immediate for the contemporary reader. The fact that he has changed the ordinary tree into a gallows tree and the barnacle into a Scot is, even for the modern reader, an imaginative twist. But the conversion to a Soland goose is not likely to arouse a great deal of excitement in us, since we already know the Styx is the Scot's destination, whether he be untransformed barnacle or converted goose.

One of the curiosities of Cleveland's considerable ability as a satirist is that his most famous poem—and the poem which alone appears in all printed collections of his work—is less exciting and less successful for the modern reader than some which are much less hailed. Understanding this difference of appeal is not terribly difficult. The prejudice which was taken as a matter of course by the conventional English critic up to our time was quite plainly against the Scotch. And, while *"The Rebell* Scot" is a considerable achievement, its chief appeal—making allowance, of course, for some very effective portions—may be in its having attacked the Scots. An understanding of English history of the period makes it simple to see why an effective attack on them would be thought wit in all ages.

An understanding of the history of the period and of Cleveland's own involvement with affairs helps us see, too, that Cleveland's gift for satire was a complex one, modulated by a number of things. One of those was the seriousness of events or their potential for serious effect. Another was the closeness of Cleveland to his subject, particularly in the poems he wrote which discuss King Charles and the odd behavior which characterized much of his negotiations with Parliament and with the Scots in the years just before hostilities broke out. In a sense, then, Cleveland is in company with most satirists who could write a general attack when occasion warranted it and a very specific attack when that seemed more appropriate.

What distinguishes Cleveland's satire is partly its ruthlessness, specifically in those poems written early in the Civil War, and partly his gift for rhetorical invention of a surprising fruitfulness. In the satires, even those which have something of the air of exercise to them, Cleveland's fantastic wit finds its fullest expression. Looking back over all his work, we can see that the most obvious development for his wit was satirical: wit for its own sake was not beneath his dignity, but wit as a weapon of war was the most dignified wit of all.

CHAPTER 6

Epistles and Characters: The Prose

I *The Problem of the Text*

THE most remarkable thing about Cleveland's prose is that it is more clearly of a piece with his poetry than anyone would expect. When we read Milton's prose, for instance, we are hardly prepared for what happens in Milton's poetry, despite the fact that some themes and concerns remain the same from one genre to the other. But the constancy of themes, or even of general concerns, is not sufficient for us to feel a profound unity from genre to genre. But, in Cleveland, as in relatively few other poets, the experience of reading the prose is really quite similar to that of reading the poetry. The tone of the prose resembles that of the poetry; the use of wit is no less profound and no less daring in the prose; the images which abound in the poetry, including those which indicate unusual reading or interest in peculiar lore, are also found in the prose. Furthermore, some of the same ends are served by both the prose and the poems, particularly by the satirical and political prose, as we might expect. But some prose, such as the already-mentioned letter to Cromwell, is most directly expressive and almost surely a vehicle of personal expression. In short, a student of Cleveland's poetry would have little difficulty in recognizing the style of his prose, particularly that which is most likely to be genuine.

And this statement brings us to the problem of texts and their reliability. As with the poems, there are numerous writers of prose who were happy to masquerade as Cleveland. If we use the poems as a stylistic touchstone, most of the spurious works can be reliably set aside. If we use Eleanor Withington's textual conclusions in regard to the poetry also for the prose, then we will trust the 1677 edition of the collected works as the most trustworthy. Withington's judgment is quite correct in my opinion, and my own procedure is to treat the works in the 1677 edition as genuine and complete and to treat the works which were not included in that edition as most likely not Cleveland's. S. V. Gapp contends that much of Cleveland's energies were spent after the surrender at Newark in preparing tirades for the underground Royalist "mercuries." The *Cambridge Bibliography of English Literature* accepts Gapp's view; but, since the evidence is scanty and the conclusions quite tenuous, the ascription of individual essays is most speculative at best. That there may be prose of Cleveland's left to be discovered is probably quite likely; but, for the moment and in the absence of any modern edition whatsoever since the seventeenth century, the most sensible method is to describe fully those works that we can most reasonably trust as Cleveland's.

Since there is no modern edition, my method is to quote liberally from the prose, and to quote especially those passages which have the most interesting implications for a reading of the poetry. The 1677 edition includes the following works in English in the following order:

The Character of a Country-Committeeman, with the Ear-mark of a Sequestrator, p. 93
The Character of a Diurnal-maker, p. 101
The Character of a London-Diurnal, p. 108
A Letter sent from a Parliament-Officer at Grantham to Mr. Cleveland in Newark, p. 119
Mr. Cleveland's Reply, p. 120
The Officer's Rejoynder, p. 123
Mr. Cleveland's Answer, p. 125
An Answer to a Pamphlet written against the Lord Digby's Speech, concerning the Death of the Earl of Strafford, p. 130
To the Protector after long and vile Durance in Prison, p. 142
To the Earl of Newcastle, p. 146
To the Earl of Holland, then Chancellour of the University of Cambridge, p. 148
To the Earl of Westmorland, p. 149
A Letter to a Friend disswading him from his Attempt to Marry a Nun, p. 153
The Piece of a Common Place upon Romans the 4th. Last Verse, p. 161
The Answer to the Newark-Summons, p. 169

After page 173, there are several typical juvenalia of the sort which often flesh out these kinds of collections: Latin orations delivered in the schools. And of the fifteen pieces which compose the

collection, two are by a "Parliament-Officer at Grantham," included
in order to give us a better sense of the meaningfulness of Cleveland's replies. Of the remaining pieces, at least one, the commentary
on Romans, is very curious for Cleveland. It is, to begin with, a
sermon written in a very elegant and smooth style; and it is quite
unlike anything else in the prose or in the poetry except for the
"Epitaph on the Earl of Strafford." Cleveland would seem odd in
the pulpit, and he would seem just as odd as the author of a piece
which could be delivered from the pulpit—even if it were never
actually delivered.

A sample of this sermon should suffice to indicate the problem of
Cleveland's authorship. One of the most striking aspects of the
entire sermon is its scrupulous attentiveness to maintaining the
metaphor without distraction—a practice untypical of Cleveland.
Furthermore, the smoothness of the sentences, with carefully bal-
anced phrases, is unlike Cleveland, though it is plainly the work of a
man trained in rhetoric. The imagery is common enough, but the
uses of consonance and assonance are rather uncommon:

> I begin with the Evening, and so I may well style the Passion, since the
> Horrour thereof turn'd Noon into Night, and made a Miracle maintain my
> metaphor. The Sun was obscur'd by Sympathy, and his Darkness points us
> to a greater Eclipse. The Sun and the Moon, what are they but Parables of
> our Saviour and the Soul of Man? The Moon is the Soul; I am sure her Spots
> will not Confute the Similitude. I might here slacken the Reigns of my
> Comparison, and show you how the Moon of her self is a dark Body, and
> what Light she partakes, she receives it from the Sun at second hand. How
> every Soul is by Nature sinful and in the Shadow of Death, till *the Light*
> *that lightens the Gentiles, till the day-spring on high visit us.* I might pursue
> my Allegory in the Eclipse. The Shadow of the Earth intercepts the Beams
> of the Sun, and so the Moon suffers an Eclipse. Pleasure and Profit, those
> two Dugs of the World, what are they but Earthly shadows that Eclipse the
> Soul, and deprive it of the sweet influence of the Sun of Righteousness. But
> I hold me to the Metaphor, my Text will warrant the Parallel. (163–64)

It is difficult to say whether such a sermon is the product of an
Anglican or of a Puritan imagination, though there may be good
reason to suspect either. If we take seriously the almost rash reference to the twin dugs of pleasure and profit, we might assume a
Puritan tract. If we take the central references to the Passion and
the elegance of the metaphors more seriously, then it seems a

Church of England tract. Even the reference to dividing texts, which Cleveland made earlier in his taunting of the zealots in the case of the *etcetera* oath, does not necessarily indicate that the work is the product of a Puritan mind. More important is the fact that it represents a link with the poetry. But here it is said with a straight face, not with a sly wink: "Consider then my Text, like the Veil of the Temple rent in twain," and "And well may my Text be divided by the Temple, since our Saviour shadowed both parts of it under that Nation" (both, 165).

But these are not the only stylistic and specific links with the poetry. One very striking sentence brings two images to mind which are both quite like Cleveland. In it, we find a clear reference to cards, which apparently amused Cleveland considerably, and to the practice of ringing church bells from the bass tones to the high tones as a sign of calamity or alarm: "Thus were all things shuffled, and Nature rung the Bells backwards, as if every Creature desir'd to bear the Burden of our Saviour's Elegy" (167). This reference to bells compares directly with the same image in two (albeit very different) poems: "Bells which ring backward in this great Combustion" (18) in "*Rupert*ismus," and "Ring the bells backward; I am all on fire" (5) in "*The Rebell* Scot." All the sermon lacks is a clear reference to fire, the occasion on which the bells most frequently were rung backward.

The most remarkable aspect of the sermon is not to be found only in such spot references, ones which probably should be taken as clear links with the poetry. But the really interesting feature of this work is that it relates so clearly to that side of Cleveland which was not the popular one. It is not a sermon in the vein that the character of the London diurnal is; it is not biting, not satirical, not a great crowd-pleaser. Rather, it is something of an exercise, perhaps even a university exercise, of the sort I have already discussed in the chapter about Cleveland's earlier lyric poems. There is no reason to suspect that Cleveland would have performed any less brilliantly on the subject of the Passion and the Resurrection than he would on the subject of a "Mixed Assembly," though we and his original audience find it more natural of him to take issue with a national circumstance and give it the whipping he felt it deserved.

Still, the precedent of such unusual poems as "Upon the Kings return from Scotland," and Epitaph on the Earl or Strafford," as well, perhaps, as "The King's Disguise," seems matched by this remarkable addition to the prose. If they do not have in common a deep sincerity, or a deep personal commitment, they do have in common the elegance of metaphoric development, the smoothness of style, and the careful rhetorical invention. There also seems to be some effort to keep the extreme inventive impulse under control. In other words, we perceive what might be described as an attempt to avoid explicit Clevelandisms while we also see a considerable effort to retain and develop those kinds of inventions which in other poems blossomed into extreme metaphors or even overblown conceits. We may consider, for instance, the following comparison of the tears which showered at the Passion with the forty days of rain which compose the Flood: "A Deluge of Grief-showers down in the Passion, but the Waters will cease, and the Dove will return with a Leaf in her mouth" (163). In comparison with the rainspouts of grief that Cleveland lavished on Edward King, this statement seems to be in remarkably close control. Yet, we can see quite clearly the urge for enlargement which expresses itself in the choice of metaphor.

The passage which follows immediately after the one quoted above is curious for several reasons. First, it does what Cleveland frequently does: it proceeds entirely by a succession of images and metaphors, moving from one to the other with what we might regard, in this case as relative unconcern rather than total abandon. Nonetheless, a great deal of ground is covered in a very short time:

> Nothing but Joy and Triumph, Pomp and Pageants at the Resurrection. But methinks St. *Paul* puts new Cloth into an old garment, mends the Rent of the Passion with the Resurrection. *Can the children of the Bride-chamber weep while the Bridegroom is with them?* While the Resurrection is in the Text, who can Tune his Soul to lament his Passion; again, by the Waters of *Babylon* is no singing the Songs of *Sion*. When Grief hath lock'd up the Heart with the story of the Passion, what Key of Mirth can let in the Anthem of the Resurrection? Different Notes you see, and yet Wee'l attempt an Harmony. *Bassus* and *Altus*, a Deep Base that must reach as low as Hell to describe the Passion, and thence rebound to a joyful *Altus*, the high-strain of the Resurrection. (163)

It is by no means difficult to imagine how this prose statement might have been handled in poetry. The sequence of image and metaphor might have remained quite similar, though the lure of end-rhyme would undoubtedly have produced an exuberance which is not present here. The hint of raggedness present in the last three sentences of the passage, with the internal "rhyme" in the next to last sentence, would probably have become more pronounced because of the ten-syllable structure any poem using this material probably would have taken.

My suggestions to this point have implied that the reason for Cleveland's being more controlled and for his using a somewhat atypical style in this somewhat atypical sermon has to do with his carefulness and his art. Perhaps that is the entire case, though perhaps it is only a part of it. There is the possibility that this early university piece was written sometime before Cleveland achieved maturity in the handling of the materials of invention.

The structure may bolster this likelihood. Ordinarily, Cleveland tends to structure his poems around the continuing effervescence of metaphor growing out of metaphor, or of comparison and instance piled on top of comparison and instance. A suggestion of this structural principle, the principle of accretion, can be seen in the passages I have quoted from the sermon. But much more important, structurally, is the entire pattern of duality: the dialectic nature of the entire sermon. As we know from reading the university prolusions, the dialectic is a very common tool of the performing student; and it is at root, too, of the Ramist skill in dichotomizing or "dividing." This sermon is structured entirely on a succession of such dialectical divisions as the Passion and the Resurrection; Good Friday and Easter; and, finally, with most lasting effect, evening and morning. At one point, Cleveland's ingenuity brings the bipartite celebrations of the Passion and the Resurrection to a kind of transcendent union by imagining them as having happened on the same day. His ingenuity is interesting if only because it forces him into a farfetched, inappropriate analogy with Greek mysteries and causes him to begin the entire sermon on a very strange note:

The Athenians had two sorts of Holy Mysteries, two distinct times, *November* and *August*, for their Celebration: but when king *Demetrius* desir'd to be admitted into their Fraternity, and see both their Solemnities at once, the People past a Decree, that the Month *March*, when the King requested it, should be call'd November, and after the Ceremonies due to that Month were finished, it should be translated to *August*, and so at the second return of this new Leap year they accomplished his Request. Two greater Mysteries are the parts of my Text, the Passion and the Resurrection; several times appropriate for either *Good Friday* or *Easter*. But as the

Athenian Decree made *November* and *August* meet in *March,* so give me
lieve by a less *Syncope* of Time to contract *Good Friday* and *Easter* both to a
day, as the Passion and Resurrection are both in my text; *Who was delivered
for our offenses,* &c. And I may the rather link them both on a day, because
the Text is willing to admit some Resemblance. The Evening and the
morning make the day, saith the Holy Spirit; the Method of my Text
observes as much: here is the Evening, the Passion, when our Saviour
strip'd himself of those Rags of Mortality, and lay down in the Bed of
Corruption, where he stays not long; but the Morning breaks in the Resurrection, *when this Corruptible shall put on Incorruption, and this Mortal
shall put on Immortality.* So then my Text is a Day from Sun to Sun, *Soles
occidere & redire possunt,* from the Sun-set of his Passion to the Sun rise of
his Resurrection. (161)

And thus, though the sermon seemed to be heading in a very
strange direction in its references to Greek mysteries, Cleveland
brings us to a fresh consideration of his basic imagery, the sun and
the day. By an act, as he says, of "syncope," they become one and
the same but still retain their literal meanings and their symbolic
associations with the Savior. The movement from one moment in
the development of the imagery is smooth; and the imagery itself,
while by no means unusual or strikingly original, is elegantly varied.
The entire sermon continues in this fashion: inventive, but
smoothly elegant. It ends, however, on a note which is somewhat
different from its beginning. Like many of Cleveland's poems, the
controlling imagery which seemed susceptible of development
throughout the poem is ultimately abandoned. The sermon, which
began with an allusion to Greek ritual and which seemed content to
focus on the religious imagery of Sun and Son, of Passion and Resurrection, turns itself around, at the last, to political rather than to
religious considerations:

The Quality of his Companions augments his Misery. He was born among
Beasts, and doth he not die so too? Man without understanding is like unto
a Beast that perisheth. Betwixt two Thieves. You see Vice to Vertue is two
to one: Vertue is in the Centre, Vice in the Circumference; vast is the
Circuit. . . . Thieves, and well too, *Barrabbas* was too good for him now;
mark but their Election; *Not him, but Barrabbas.* But methinks his Crown
might command a Distance; but 'tis a Crown of Thorns: and if you consider
well the Troubles annex'd to a Crown, it may seem a *Tautology.* Every
Crown is a Crown of Thorns. See here Cruelty Quartering her Arms with
Division. . . . They Crown him, but 'tis for Sacrifice. They never acknowl-
edge him King of the Jews, till upon the Cross, that so his Title might set off
his Misery. (168)

At root, the catachresis of the circumstances intrigues Cleveland; and the catachresis relates to the dialectic of the opening passages in form and structure, if not in subject. The closing passages have what the opening passages do not: the addition of irony. There is nothing ironic about conjoining the Passion and the Resurrection, though there is indeed something witty about the compression. But the ironic juxtaposition of the crown of the king of the Jews being placed on the head of Jesus only when he is hanged like a thief on a cross is the point of the final passages of the sermon. Cleveland states the point succinctly in the sentence relating to heraldry: "Cruelty Quartering her Arms with Division." For an instant, Christ on the Cross is an emblem for a shield (we think of Godfrey of Boulogne in "Upon Sir Thomas Martin," whose arms were five golden crosses on a field of silver); but the shield represents the arms not of a knight but of Cruelty personified. Such irony as Cleveland refers to can be the work only of such a figure as catachresis.

The emblematic quality of this entire final passage is somewhat remarkable. Vice and virtue take their usual emblematic stances, and all the action seems "stopped" in order for us to examine the tableau of Christ on the cross—with an eye, of course, to the ironies implied in the arrangement of the circumstances. A very peculiar moment, it is perhaps less so when we consider that it is one prepared for us not by men merely but by the abstraction Cruelty.

It is hard to imagine the circumstances which might have prevailed upon Cleveland to compose such a sermon. But, then, it is hard to imagine him having written some of the poems of apparently straightforward and sincere personal passion which he did. What does seem reasonable to assume is that, if Cleveland had written a sermon early in his career, this would certainly be the kind of production he would have written. Although this piece has some of the odor of a school exercise about it, it also contains suggestions of Cleveland's later development: the elaboration of metaphor, the general rhetorical inventiveness, and the use of specific images and specific expressions which appear elsewhere.

Certain other of Cleveland's writings which do not appear in the 1677 edition but which, for various reasons not always clear, are ascribed to him are worth mentioning. One is *Majestas Intemperata or, The Immortality of the King,* a fifty-six page tract published in 1649. Nothing in the tract itself suggests anything about its possible authorship and the chances of its having been written by Cleveland seem remote in view of the confidence the author has in the reign of

Charles II. Cleveland died without genuine cause to think Charles would ever be made king of England. The entire tract makes a strong plea for the desirability of having a king as head of government, and it shows in the course of a quasi-legal history of England that Cromwell and Richard Rich are made of the same rotten stuff. The piece ends with, "if there be any Justice any where, the innocency of the *holiest Martyrs* quarrel shall prevail, and from the day of that accursed *Regicide, CHARLES* the Second's Crown shall flourish." The sympathies are probably close to those of Cleveland, but the likelihood that he wrote the tract is not great.

In Berdan's appendix D, which has information on more prose works attributed to Cleveland, he comments about the chances of the works' authenticity. He has reason to be doubtful of all prose works which do not appear in the 1677 edition. His appendix also gives some useful information about the printing history of the several works. One long work which found its way into the 1687 edition is "The Idol of the Clowns, or the Insurrection of Wat the Tyler," a work first published in 1654 and 1658. In the 1699 edition it is titled, "The Rustick Rampant." It apparently had some popularity, but it is stylistically very different from any of the prose or the poetry which can easily be authenticated. For one thing, it is a very lengthy treatment of a theme which never figures in any of the poems or authenticated prose. It is hardly likely that a writer like Cleveland, who repeats so much from one work to another, would write a tract which is more than a hundred pages in length and about a character so controversial as Wat the Tyler and then never mention him again. Berdan suggests that one Francis White of Gray's Inn may have been the author, though it seems safe to say that, tradition notwithstanding, Cleveland is not a good candidate for its authorship. Another work, *Midsummer-Moone, or Lunacy Rampant,* which appeared in a "Cleveland Revived" edition, has been also attributed to F. Cheynell; first published in 1648, it is quite unlike Cleveland in style.

II   *The Unmistakable Cleveland*

A piece which, on the other hand is quite distinctly in the style of Cleveland—in fact, unmistakably so—is "The Character of a Country-Committeeman, with the Ear-mark of a Sequestrator." This work appears not only in the 1677 edition, but in earlier editions, beginning with an edition of 1651. Cleveland had dealt with the problem of sequestration in "Upon Sir Thomas Martin," and some of the themes he used in this work reappear in the "Character." Of course, we have no way of telling for certain how much time might have lapsed between the two works or how early the "Character" might have been written before it was printed. The strong likelihood is that it, like many other of Cleveland's works, circulated in manuscript for a time before it was printed.

One of the immediately familiar notes is struck in the effort to use the name, the Country-Committeeman, as witness of outrage: the problem of plurality (committee being a number of men) in singularity (man being one only). Thus, a "Committee-man" by Cleveland's definition is a monstrous thing, just as Sir Thomas Knights was himself derided for his singular plurality. The very name has "number enough in it to make an Epithet for Legion. . . . It is a well truss'd Title that contains both the Number and the Beast; for a Committee-man is a Noun of multitude" (93). The analysis is characteristic of Cleveland in that it has a methodical approach—a combination of grammar and etymology—and it analyzes the number of the word while also examining its meaning. The method is used to some advantage in Milton's *De Doctrina Christiana*, as well as in many other documents of the period; therefore, we can recognize the method as a standard approach common to writer and audience.

The character defines the committee-man, then, by his plurality. Then it proceeds to conjure up some other examples of plurality with which to compare the committee-man. None of them are complimentary, of course. Cleveland begins with a comparison with the Pope and his triple tiara, the three-part crown which graces his head at solemn ceremonies. This comparison is even more odious than it seems at first since Cleveland is accusing the committee-man of arrogating unto himself the powers not just of religious tyranny, but of the brand of it that England most dreaded. Again, echoes of Milton's "new priest writ large" suggest themselves, just as do echoes of Cleveland's other protests. He accuses the committee-man of not removing kingship from England but of multipling it across the land like a plague. Where there was but one, there is now a legion:

here is the Plurality of Crowns to one Head, joyn them together and there is a Harmony in Discord. The Tripleheaded Turn-key of Heaven with the Tripleheaded Porter of Hell. A Committee-man is the Reliques of Regal

Government, but, like Holy Reliques, he outbulks the Substance whereof he is a Remnant. There is a score of Kings in a Committee, as in the Reliques of the Cross there is the number of twenty. This is the gyant with the hundred hands that wields the Scepter; the Tyrannical Bead-Roll by which the Kingdom prays backward, and at every Curse drops a Committee-man. Let *Charles* be wav'd, whose condescending Clemency aggravates the Defection, and make *Nero* the Question, better a *Nero* than a Committee. There is less Execution by a single Bullet, than by Case-shot. (93–94)

In typical fashion we have come from the Pope to St. Peter in Heaven, to Cerberus in Hell, through relics and rosaries, to Charles and Nero. Charles was so soft and yielding a king that to imagine a comparison of him with a committee-man would put the latter at too awful a disadvantage. Rather, a committee-man should be considered as an alternative to a Nero, a genuine tyrant; for, in such a comparison, the committee-man would have a better chance to fare well. But, as Cleveland argues, not even such a comparison can help the committee-man.

The play with grammatical number is so characteristic of Cleveland as to be recognized immediately. Part of the delight that a contemporary reader would have derived from such a burst of wit comes from the fact that such a normally innocuous diversion of grammatical analysis (though it has a worthy medieval rabbinical history in exegesis) can produce such a virulent attack. In Cleveland's hand, such analysis begets more analysis, more scrutiny, more examples, and more witty opportunities.

His character continues to expand, with a kind of emblem in the making. Instead of describing the committee-man physically— though the term "ear-mark" in the title is a dig at the normally prominent ears of the Puritan Roundheads—Cleveland draws his figure as if he were represented in Alciati or Ripa as a standard emblem. "Now a Committee man is a party-colour'd Officer. He must be drawn like *Janus* with Cross and Pile in his Countenance; as he relates to the Souldiers, or faces about to his fleecing the Country" (94). The irony is plain in that the committee-man has the forces of religion (in the Cross), and of the Puritan forms of religion, and of the army (in the Pile or javelin). As a military man he is something of a fool: party-colored like a jester. As a religious man, he is a curious shepherd: fleecing the country. A pleasant and amusing ironic sequence, it is built again on the dialectical foundation inherent in the two-faced Janus himself: one face of ire; one face of devotion. Such hypocrisy was the most constant charge leveled against the Puritans.

But the committee-man is not merely a hypocrite—such an accusation would not be strong enough—he is accused of serving his own people badly. His job is to scour the country to raise funds for the service, to sequester the estates of those who are not in support of Parliament, thence to deliver the funds and use them for the general purpose of support. But, the committee-man has other ideas: "The Country people beeing like an *Irish* Cow that will not give down her Milk, unless she see her Calf before her: Hence it is he is the Garrison's Dry-Nurse, he chews their Contributions before he feeds them; so the poor Souldiers live like *Trochilus* by picking the teeth of this sacred Crocodile" (95–96).

The military aspect, we discover, can almost be considered the benevolent aspect of the committee-man. But there is then the more curious aspect of the taxing committee-man: he squeezes his magnified tithes out of the most innocent of the country-dwellers. The imagery becomes appropriately fundamental, if Freud is correct in associating money and feces, and is mildly reminiscent of "The Mixed Assembly." To be sure, it is not a surprising side of Cleveland which we see:

So much for his Warlike or Ammunition-Face, which is so preternatural, that it is rather a Vizard than a Face; *Mars* in him hath but a blinking Aspect, his Face of Arms is like his Coat, *Partie per pale*,[1] Souldier and Gentleman much of a scantling.

Now enter his Taxing and deglubing Face, a squeezing Look, like that of *Vespasianus*, as if he were bleeding over a Close-stool.

Take him thus, and he is in the Inquisition of the Purse an Authentic Gypsie, that nips your Bung with a Canting Ordinance: not a murthered Fortune in all the Country but bleeds at the Touch of this Malefactor. He is the Spleen of the Body Politick that swells it self to the Consumption of the Whole. At first indeed he Ferreted for the Parliament, but since he hath got off his Cope, he set up for himself. He lives upon the Sins of the People, and that is a good standing Dish too. (96)

We must admit that a considerable portion of humor is present in the description of the "deglubing," or flaying, face of the taxing man as similar to that of Vespasian over a close-stool. There is the sense of indignity about it, the sense of unnaturalness, the sense of strain, and finally the implication of bleeding the country dry. Furthermore, we can get a sense of Cleveland's outrage by the scatological indulgences which mark the passage—as, for example, we could measure the intensity of outrage in the poems often by the same means. There comes a time when nothing that can be imagined is too ripe for use against the subject in question.

Cleveland describes the committee-man as merciless and unduly cruel in the discharging of his duties. "He alienes a Delinquent's Estate with as little Remorse, as his other Holiness gives away an Heretick's Kingdom; and for the truth of his Delinquency, both Chapmen have as little share of Infallibility" (97). He also accuses Parliament of having continued the Star Chamber under its own rule of arbitrary government, and he asserts that things have not changed in the ways in which they could profitably have done. The courts that take a delinquent's estate from him are as rigged and bloodthirsty as any of the worst that could be found under royalty. "Lye," he says immediately after the passage quoted above, "is the Grand Salad of Arbitrary Government, Executor to the Star chamber and the High Commission; for those Courts are not extinct, they survive in him, like Dollars changed into single Money."

The few pages which remain describe the committee-man in terms of comparisons which constantly compromise him. He is a "Dutch Hotch-Potch," and he is like a familiar of witches. His sequestrator is "the States Cormorant, one that fishes for the publick, but feeds himself. . . . There are more Monsters retain to him, than to all the Limbs in Anatomy." And, finally, he realizes that his reader, like himself, is beginning to grow weary of this tiresome creature; therefore, he brings his character to a close. His final charge is that the committee-man has struck at the roots of civilization: paternity and its succession. In this blow he has hit Cleveland and Cleveland's party where they are most concerned and where they are most vulnerable. The entire Royalist cause depends on such succession; so, when Cleveland ends his portrait by saying, "for he ruines the Father, beggars the Son, and strangles the hopes of all Posterity" (101), he delivers, in fact, his final blow. It should be his most telling.

As a character, this portrait has some curious features. For one, its appeal is highly intellectual; and its concepts are relatively abstract. The moments of physical description are few, with the most exacting moments being essentially emblematic in quality.

The character is told in terms of behavior and then in terms of ultimate effects. The committee-man is a person of consequence, and this character details all the consequences.

III *Character as Anatomy*

In "The Character of a Diurnal-Maker," Cleveland is not so quick to abandon visual description and visual taunts. In fact, at one point Cleveland begins to anatomize his victim, beginning with the head and proceeding to the toes in a quite conscious dissection. But he begins by developing an invidious comparison in which the diurnal-maker is compared with a historian for what is generally not a bad reason, though the comparison is fundamentally unfair. The diurnal, a prototype of our newspaper, appeared fairly regularly, though by no means daily, and one of its principal purposes was to keep Englishmen informed on the progress of international events. In ages past, chroniclers like Holinshed and the classical historians performed similar services in that they kept track of events and helped people see events in some historical perspective. The modern English diurnal developed from models in Holland, where many Englishmen lived and worked. The development was aided somewhat by English licensing laws which prohibited certain kinds of news from being printed in England. It was not long before the political usefulness of such journals was recognized, and they became the instruments of attack of both the Royalists and the Parliamentarians.

Thus, the character opens with a bristling array of comparisons:

A Diurnal-maker is the Sub-almoner of History, Queen *Mab's* Register, one whom, by the same Figure that a North country Pedlar is a Merchant-man, you may style an Author. It is like overreach of Language, when every Thin, tinder-cloak'd Quack must be called a Doctor; when a clumsie Cobler usurps the Attribute of our English Peers and is vamp'd a Translator. List him a Writer, and you smother *Geoffrey* in Swabber-slops; the very name of Dabler over-sets him; he is swallowed up in the phrase, like Sir. *S. L.* in a great Saddle, nothing to be seen, but the Ciddy Feather in his Crown. They call him a Mercury, but he becomes the Epithet, like the little Negro mounted upon an Elephant, just such another Blot Rampant. (101–2)

The diurnal-maker is a servant of history, not a master of it, any more than he is fit for anything other than to follow Mab, queen of

the fairies, and make fairy tales. He is like a poor man wrapped in
the garb of a peer: like Sly in *Taming of the Shrew*, he is still an
impoverished nobody. It is not absolutely essential that Cleveland
compare the average diurnal-maker with Geoffrey Chaucer, though
the comparison of the figure the diurnal-maker cuts is certainly
compared amusingly with Sir Samuel Luke (the most probable candidate for *S. L.* of the passage), who is often regarded as the model
for the hero of Samuel Butler's satire on the Puritans, *Hudibras*.

Other comparisons are not quite so controlled. Once things get
going, Cleveland says, "The silly Country-man, who seeing an Ape
in a Scarlet-coat, bless'd his young Worship, and gave his Landlord
joy of the hopes of his House, did not slander his Complement with
worse Application, than he that names this Shred an Historian"
(102). And, "Such an Historian would hardly pass muster with a
Scotch Stationer in a Sieveful of Ballads and Godly Books." He
continues, "I have heard of Puppets that could prattle in a Play, but
never saw of their Writings before" (103), and he completes the
slander with "Not a Worm that gnaws on the dull Scalp of Volumi-
nous *Hollinshed*, but at every Meal devour's more Chronicle, than
his Tribe amounts to."

Much of the brief diatribe is couched in terms of such comparisons and instances, again reminding us of the basic technique used
in the poems. Instance follows instance, and each helps give authority to the ones that preceded it. The logic is nothing new, but it is
limited in its appeal to those people and those times which recognize a metaphoric mode of thought as an effective means of reasoning. The metaphor by itself does the convincing. The diurnal-maker
is measured by metaphor: each comparison shows him how low he
is, how unable he is to "Stack up" against even such examples of
lowliness as a bookworm lunching on a chronicle of days past. The
comparisons proliferate seemingly on their own and without a
"grand design," and such a technique again is what we would expect.

Cleveland does use some of the conventional approaches that we
would expect from the character, particularly those which depend
on careful description. He begins one paragraph with, "And here I
think it it [*sic*] were not amiss to take a particular how he is ac-
coutred, and so do by him as he in his *Siquis* for the Wall-ey'd Mare,
or the Crop Flea-bitten, give you the Marks of the Beast" (105). He
begins with "his Head, which is ever in Clouts, as if the Night-cap

should make *Affidavit,* that the Brain was pregnant," and rapidly proceeds to the ears, a favorite subject of all those who took the Puritans to task: "There's no proportion between that Head and Appurtenances. . . . In what a puzzling Neutrality is the poor Soul that moves betwixt two such ponderous Biasses?" (106). Cleveland continues in a systematic vein, moving from ears to gloves to boots. Finally, he says, "But I must draw to an end; for every Character is an Anatomy-lecture, and it fares with me in this of the Diurnal-maker, as with him that reads on a begg'd Malefactor, my Subject smells before I have gone thorow with him" (107). He leaves his dissected cadaver of a diurnal-maker to the hunters of carrion and moves on, satisfied that he has not only laid him bare to attack but has flayed him through and through.

IV　*The Character of the London Diurnal*

The most celebrated attack on the "mercuries" of the day was not this one, of course, but the first of Cleveland's important published work. "The Character of a London-Diurnal," as I have already mentioned, catapulted Cleveland to prominence in 1644. An extremely heated libel of Parliament-men and an attack on the Puritan diurnals, it is filled with images and references which appear in a number of the poems. The argument of the piece depends, to an extent, on some of the same premises developed in the character of the diurnal-maker himself, though that piece came later. The fact that the diurnal is a poor excuse for a history is played upon with apparently little immediate understanding of the real potential of the early newspaper for recording things as they happen rather than interpreting events.

To be sure, Cleveland, like many of his Royalist allies, recognized the potential of the diurnal for propagandizing, and eventually they used it for that purpose. What the Royalists did see very quickly was the power of the diurnal for attack, and Cleveland's own attack on the Puritan papers has actually something of the air of defense to it: it is the reaction of one who himself has been stung. Until later, the Royalists did not begin to make the same use of the diurnals that their adversaries did; and, by the time the "mercuries" were enlisted in their aid, their cause had been formally lost on the battlefield. But, oddly, most of Cleveland's attack is made on the grounds of the paper's being in bad form, of its not living up to its reputation as a chronicle: a misunderstanding that was probably costly to the Royalist cause.

Cleveland's attack is immediately recognizable. It is belittling and dazzling:

A Diurnal is a puny Chronicle, scarce Pin-feather'd with the wings of Time. It is a History in Sippets: The English Iliads in a Nutshel: The Apocryphal Parliament's Book of *Maccabees* in single sheets. It would tire a Welshman to reckon up how many *Aps* 'tis removed from an Annal: for it is of that Extract, only of the younger House, like a Shrimp to a Lobster. The Original Sinner in this kind was Dutch, *Gallobelgicus* the Protoplast, and the modern *Mercuries* but *Hans en kelders*. The Countess of *Zealand* was brought to bed of an Almanack, as many Children as days in the year. It may be the Legislative Lady is of that Linage, so she spawns the Diurnals, and they at *Westminster* take them in Adoption by the names of *Scoticus, Civicus, Britannicus*. In the Frontispiece of the old Beldam Diurnal, like the Contents of the Chapter, sitteth the House of Commons judging the twelve Tribes of *Israel*. You may call them the Kingdóms Anatomy before the weekly Kalendar; for such is a Diurnal, the day of the Month with what Weather in the Commonwealth. It is taken for the Pulse of the Body Politick, and the Emperick Divines of the Assembly, those Spiritual Dragooners, thumb it accordingly. Indeed it is a pretty *Synopsis;* and those Grave *Rabbies* (though in the point of Divinity) trade in no larger Authors. The Country-carrier, when he buyes it for the Vicar, miscals it the Urinal; yet properly enough, for it casts the Water of the State ever since it staled Blood. It differs from an *Aulicus*, as the Devil and his Exorcist, or as a black Witch doth from a white one, whose office is to unravel her Enchantments. (108–9)

The *Aulicus* in question is the benign Puritan "mercury," *Mercurius Aulicus*, a relative of the *Mercurius Pragmaticus* which S. V. Gapp feels Cleveland probably edited after 1647. The carrier's fanciful pronunciation—making "Urinal" out of "Diurnal"—is a comic twist which Cleveland is totally ready to exploit, just as he is ready to exploit the Dutch origins of the newspaper in the *Mercurius Gallobelgicus* by using one of his favorite images: the "Hans-in-keldar" is a phrase of the day for an unborn child that literally means "Hans in the cellar"; and the image further belittles the efforts of the beginning of the newspaper. "Staling," or urinating, blood, is the mark of a disease, one from which the whole country metaphorically suffered. Cleveland is quite right in ascribing the beginning of the newspaper to the *Gallobelgicus* since copies of it dating from 1594

still exist and it seems the earliest of the newspapers. Its "Proto-plast" seems also to have been Janson of Cologne, a "Dutchman."
Other details mark this tirade as clearly Cleveland's: the refer-ence to the Welsh pedigree, as in his similar reference in "Smec-tymnuus, *or The Club-Divines*" (4), as well as the other refer-ences to falconry, the book of Maccabees, and the legendary prodi-giousness of the woman who supposedly gave birth to a child every day for a year. Such bits of information, true or apocryphal, were bound to catch Cleveland's imagination. The fact is, this opening passage stamps the entire composition as so definitely Cleveland's as to be remarkable. The prose and poetry fed on each other to an astounding degree.

The character of the diurnal was probably enthusiastically re-ceived for its outright slander as much as for anything else. English satire has so long been distinguished by its personal attack that we tend to read such a piece as this one and forget that there was little or any literature like it before its time. But Cleveland names names—or at least initials, as in his attack on "Sir W. E.," who "looks like a Man-Midwife, not yet delivered of so much as a Cush-ion" (110). He attacks Pym on the same page by name and then indites a number of other Parliament men: "Thus a zealous Botcher in *Moorfields*, while he he [sic] was contriving some Quirpocut of Church Government, by the help of his outlying Ears and the *Otacousticon* of the Spirit, discovered such a Plot, that *Selden* in-tends to combat Antiquity, and maintain it was a Taylor's Goose that preserv'd the Capitol." The "Otacousticon" is the inner ear which hears the inner voice from which the inner light derives.

Cleveland is ruthlessly witty in this passage, which suggests that the inner lights of a Moorfields butcher can cause a world-famous scholar like John Selden to reexamine antiquity to find grounds for defending a preposterous position. This blow at the core of Puritanism exposes some of the customary anti-intellectualism of most extreme religious sects, Puritanism not the least among them.

In the process of attacking individuals, Cleveland also manages to strike at another aspect of the diurnal which originally excited his attack: its tendency to embroider the truth, or to sometimes lie outright about events. It was a favorite Parliamentary trick to un-cover plots which had been begun by themselves: "Thus the *Quixots* of the Age fight with the Windmils of their own heads, quell Monsters of their own Creation, make Plots, and then discover them, as who fitter to unkennel the Fox than the Tarrier that is part of him?" (112). He expands the attack as he becomes more specific:

I'll present them in their order. And first as a Whistler before the show enter *Stamford*, one that trod the Stage with the first, travers'd his ground, made a Leg and *Exit*. The Country people took him for one that by Order of the Houses was to dance a Morrice through the West of *England*. Well, he's a nimble Gentlemen; set him upon *Banks* his Horse in a Saddle rampant, and it is a great question which part of the Centaure shows better tricks.

....

This Cubit and half of Commander, by the help of a Diurnal routed his Enemies fifty miles off. It's strange you'll say, and yet 'tis generally believ'd he would as soon do it at that distance as nearer hand. Sure it was his Sword for which the Weapon-salve was invented; that so wounding and healing (like loving Correlates) might both work at the same removes. But the Squib is run to the end of the Rope: Room for the prodigy of Valour. Madam *Atropos* in Breeches, *Waller's* Knight errantry; and because every Mountebank must have his *Zany*, throw him *Hazelrig* to set off his Story. These two, like *Bel* and the *Dragon*, are always worshipped in the same Chapter; they hunt in couples, what one doth at the head, the other scores up at the heels.

Thus they kill a man over and over, as *Hopkins* and *Sternhold* murder the Psalms with another of the same; one chimes all in, and then the other strikes up as the Saints-Bell.

I wonder for how many Lives my Lord *Hopton* took the Lease of his Body.

First *Stamford* slew him, then *Waller* outkill'd that half a Barr; and yet it is thought the sullen Corps would scarce bleed were both these Manslayers never so near it.

....

This is the *William* whose Lady is the Conquerour; This is the City's Champion and the Diurnals delight; he that Cuckolds the General in his Commission; for he Stalks with *Essex*, and shoots under his belly, because his Excellency himself is not charged there; yet in all this triumph there is a Whip and a Bell; translate but the Scene to *Roundway Down*, there *Hazelrig's* Lobsters turned Crabs and crawled backwards; there poor Sir *William* ran to his Lady for an use of Consolation. (112–14)

Thus Cleveland loses sight somewhat of the diurnal whose character he is portraying for the opportunity to chase after some of the chief characters who appeared in its pages. Sir William Waller, commanding with Essex, did indeed aid in slowing down Sir Ralph Hopton when Hopton was commanding the king's troops as they prepared to lay siege to London. The London train-bands held themselves together, at least in appearance, at Turnham Green and forced Hopton and Charles to veer and ultimately attempt the ill-fated siege of Gloucester. Whatever the exaggerated claims were that the diurnals constantly made, the facts indicate that Hopton was baffled and the king's cause was actually lost in these early skirmishes.

The tendency of the diurnals was to claim more than was reasonable, and such a claim probably had a healthy psychological effect at the time, buoying up morale and winning allegiances—undoubtedly the reason that Cleveland attacks them so viciously. Stinging Sir Arthur Haselrig—one of Cleveland's frequent victims and one of the five Parliamentarians that King Charles sought by special warrant—was almost second nature for Cleveland. And the jibes at Sir William Waller, who soon came to be called William the Conqueror, are particularly noteworthy in view of Waller's initial effectiveness at the time of the campaigns Cleveland is concerned with. Roundway Down (July 13, 1643) was a highly important victory for Charles since it prevented Waller and Essex from threatening the stronghold at Oxford, which at that moment looked somewhat less than secure. It apparently also made possible the taking of Bristol by the Royalist forces under Prince Rupert.

At Roundway Down, Waller was faced by Ralph Hopton, an old friend, though it was the reinforcements from Oxford which ultimately undid Waller's cause. Hopton continued the campaigh, trying for some months to join forces of the Western and Northern armies for an attempt on London, according to the king's plans. The ultimate approach, much delayed, failed primarily for want of men: thus Turnham Green was a victory of numbers and of confrontation rather than a genuine battle. Waller never truly recovered his powers after Roundway Down, and he ultimately fell under arrest shortly after Pride's Purge slimmed the number of Parliamentarians from about two hundred to under sixty members. The purge in December, 1648, was to eliminate all Parliamentarians who were possibly faithful to the old cause and to the then captured king. Interestingly enough, the man who helped Colonel Pride and his troops isolate those suspected of treason was Lord Grey of Groby, the *"Stamford"* that Cleveland also accuses of being a manslayer of Hopton. It is a mild irony that Waller should have proved ultimately untrustworthy by Parliament after Cleveland attacked him so soundly.

Of course, these men are in the end to be considered as nothing more than small fry. Cleveland set his sights on Cromwell, too, though it is very unlikely that he ever foresaw the day when he would be writing to "Noll" in an effort to gain his freedom from prison. Still, Cromwell was a man to be taken seriously, particularly by those who, like Cleveland, were university men, since Cromwell contributed to the dismantling of the university chapels and took possession of Cambridge entirely. Cromwell probably does not get the attention that he would have if Cleveland had been able to foresee events, but he does get a rather vicious appraisal: "Believe him as he whistles to his *Cambridge*-Teem of Committee-men, and he doth wonders. But holy Men, like the holy Language, must be read backwards. They rifle Colleges to promote Learning, and pull down Churches for Edification. But Sacrilege is entail'd upon him. There must be a Cromwell for Cathedrals as well as Abbeys; a secure sin, whose offence carries its pardon in its mouth: for how shall he be hang'd for Church-robbery, that gives himself the benefit of the Clergy?" (116).

Curiously enough, Cleveland compares Cromwell with Edward Montague, Lord Manchester, who commanded an army along with Essex and Waller. His comparison is at the expense of Cromwell: "compar'd to *Manchester*, he is but like the Vigils to an Holy day" (116), when later events actually showed Cromwell to be much the superior in political influence and in military skill. Manchester lost his army when he was forced to resign under attack by Cromwell and others through the sweeping self-denying ordinance in which officers were required to turn back their commissions so. that the New Model Army could be formed.

Actually, Essex, Manchester, and Denbigh (also a commander at that time) forsook their commands before settlement of the ordinance. But the interesting thing is that, while Cleveland does not actually conceive such a turn of events, what he does conceive is the character of the New Model Army as it was to be under Cromwell, with its religious diffusion and its vast number of Independents. He describes Cromwell's soldiers:

Indeed as the Angels each of them makes a several Species; so every one of his Soldiers makes a distinct Church. Had these Beasts been to enter into the Ark, it would have puzzled *Noah* to have sorted them in pairs. If ever there were a Rope of Sand, it was so many Sects twisted into an Association.

They agree in nothing but that they are all Adamites in understanding. It is a sign of a Coward to wink and fight, yet all their Valour procceds from their Ignorance. (116–17)

He also charges Cromwell with having been the spawn of the devil: "he might vary the Text, and say to Corruption, *"Thou art my Father."* Then, Cleveland showers vitriol: "This is he that put out one of the Kingdom's Eyes by clouding our Mother University; and (if this Scotch Mist farther prevail) he will extinguish the other. He hath the like quarrel to both, because both are strung with the same Optick Nerve, Knowing Loyalty. Barbarous Rebel ! who will be reveng'd upon all Learning, because his Treason is beyond the Mercy of the Book (117).

A few other individuals are treated almost *en passant:* Sir William Brereton commanded a local force and aided Fairfax, also mentioned by Cleveland, in destroying the army brought by Lord Byron from Ireland at the battle of Nantwich; Sir John Gell extracted money from the people under King Charles and continued the same practice under Parliament. Of them Cleveland says, "two of *Mars* his Petty toes, such sniveling Cowards, that it is a favour to call them so" (118).

The, finally, Cleveland returns to his express subject, the diurnal: "I will close up all thus. The Victories of the Rebels are like the Magical Combat of *Apuleis,* who thinking he had slain three of his Enemies, found them at last but a Triumvirate of Bladders. Such, and so empty are the Triumphs of a Diurnal, but so many Impostumated Phancies, so many Bladders of their own blowing" (119). This felicitous reference to *The Golden Ass* includes the pun on the word bladder: "blatter," or "page," not to mention the pun on blowing and noisemaking. But Cleveland is still not primarily attacking the diurnals as much as he is attacking those who figure prominently in their pages. His character is then a character of not just the diurnals but of those foes whose work has been treated in them. In this sense, Cleveland's commentary is something like a chronicle whose purpose is to expose the characters of the chief participants in historical events—something not unlike the practice of nineteenth-century historians like John Heneage Jesse. The exception, naturally; is that Cleveland is masterful in his sniping at, and whipping of, those persons, and his purpose is more plainly to ridicule and expose than it is to inform.

The modern reader must admire Cleveland for his ability to deal with those figures who have remained prominent even in the eyes of subsequent historians. Of course Cleveland was always given credit for being a prophetic poet, so it may be the judgment of his peers was earned not by magic but by good judgment and prescience. His attack on Cromwell, for instance, shows remarkable vision in the light of later developments. His understanding of the value of the victory at Roundway Down is also an example of his appreciation of the importance of events; for though it was no Marston Moor, it was one of the more genuinely crucial battles of the early campaign years.

The contemporary reader must have been delighted at the pithiness of Cleveland's attacks on such prominent men. Few such readers could ever have enjoyed as literate a libel as the character of the diurnal affords them. Certainly that libel carries over into Cleveland's later verse, but there are moments in which the power and incisiveness of the prose far outdoes anything in the poetry. Even "The Rebell Scot" is rarely bitterer than the indictment of Cromwell, the clouder of "our Mother University." What the prose lacks is compression and the surprise of rhyme, but it lacks none of the outrage and none of the acidulousness of satirical attack. Cleveland's claim to being the first satirist is irrelevant, but he certainly deserves credit, if that is a reasonable word here, for dramatically expanding the possibilities of satire. Historians might claim with a high degree of validity that it was the times, the wars of the press which preceded and accompanied the wars of the politicians and armies, that produced such satire. Such times and the access to such weapons as a bustling press undoubtedly gave ample opportunity for expression of personal spleen, but few examples were of the quality and ingenuity of Cleveland's until the Restoration.

V   *Epistles and Minor Moments*

The rest of Cleveland's prose offers little that is of the same character, even in part, as the exercise on the London diurnal. And except for a reply to an attack on Lord Digby, the Royalist who spoke against the decision to execute Strafford, the remainder of the works are letters of one variety and another. A batch which is curious primarily for its wit-play in the heat of military preparations is the exchange of letters between Cleveland in his role of Judge-Advocate of Newark and a Parliamentary officer identified as W. E.

at Grantham. It seems that one of the officer's servants, named Hill, defected to the fortifications at Newark with £133 8d. The officer wrote in hopes that Cleveland would act on principle and send the servant to be punished and return the money to its rightful owner. The officer writes as if he knew Cleveland's reputation as a wit, for he loses no opportunity to pun:

This precise Sum I was willing you should know, supposing your Wisdom might own the moneys, though your Honesty could hardly allow the Act: which if so, and that hereafter we shall find it no Sin to violate your Sanctuary, and upon the Audit find the Receit, we may happily count it a Loan, and not a Loss, it being in hands responsible for greater matters. And now, Sir, let me speak to you as a Judge, not as an Advocate. Give the Fellow his just reward; prefer him, or send him hither: if you dare not Trust him, let him be Trussed. (120)

Cleveland's response is filled with biblical and classical references which echo those scattered through the officer's letter, and he assaults the officer's style:

I perceive your Communication is not always Yea, Yea; now and then a little Harlotry-Rhetorick. You say that your Man is entred our Ark: I am sorry you were so ignorant in Scripture, as to let him come single. The Text had been better satisfied, if you had pleased to bear him company; for then the Beasts had entred by Couples: But though he came alone, yet well lined it seems, with 133 *I. 8d.* Sure your Hue and Cry hath good Lungs, it would have been out of breath else, before it had reached the Eight pence. (121)

In all of this diatribe the sight of the man and his treasure is almost lost. Cleveland has an opportunity for scathing a saint directly, and he does so with delight and relish. The ultimate judgment he makes is that it is too bad, though nonetheless essential, that he must refuse to be judge of one "Hill," and instead be his advocate and offer him protection. In the torrent of wit which expresses such a conclusion, the point itself is virtually lost; and the issue soon shifts to wit as opposed to thievery. "The Officer's Rejoynder" is a bit of amusement in itself, and shows no small ability at wit:

Had not Indulgent Mercy provided for troubled Spirits Sacred Oracles, how troubled had you been to contrive something worthy of Laughter? How easie had the Expence of your Wit been trussed up in an Egg-shell. I dare not trace in holy Ground, it is not safe nibbling there. You see what

Doctrine I make of your Use; but yet so far as yours is Profane give me lieve
to nibble at Wit. Though I dare not undertake like a mighty Coloss (whose
very motion doth Cleave Land, like *Terram findere*) to devour indigested
lumps of Wit, as the *Cyclops* Men at a Morsel, and then retail it out, as a
Juggler doth Inkle, by the Yard. (123)

How land's end cleaves land is never fully explained, and Cleveland is quick in calling the officer's attention to that in his subsequent attack. But in this, the officer's rejoinder, we see the
officer, apparently fully aware of the nature and reputation of his
correspondent, paying virtually no attention at all to the matters
pressing at hand, but giving himself over to the exercise of invention
as if it would be a considerable victory indeed to subdue one of the
king's wits in such mock battle. And, if nothing else, the officer
piques Cleveland, and causes him to answer almost point for point,
in this manner:

Certainly your spirit is troubled, else your Expression had not run so mud-
dy; for never was Oracle more ambiguous, if possible to be reconciled to
Sence. The Wit which you say may be truss'd up in an Egg shell, I fear your
Oval Crown hath scarce Capacity enough to contain. You disclaim being a
Coloss; Content; I have as diminitive thoughts of you as you please. I take
you for a Jack-a-Lent, and my Pen shall make use of you accordingly, three
Throws for a penny. But you cannot Cleave Land like *Terram Findere*.
What a chargeable Commodity is Wit at *Grantham* where the poor Writer
plays the Pimp, and jumbles two Languages together in unlawful Sheets for
the Production of a Quibble: but I applaud your Cunning, for the more
unknown Tongue you jest in, your wit will be the better. And why cannot
you Cleave the Land? Tread but hard, and your cloven Foot will leave its
Impression. You talk of *Cyclops* & Jugglers (indeed hard words are the
Juggler's Dialect:) But take heed, the time may come, when unless you can
play *Presto* be gone, your Run away King may cause you Juggler wise to
disgorge your Fate, and vomit a Rope instead of Inkle. (126–27)

Actually, Cleveland returns in this final note in the battle of wit to
the proper subject of the debate, Hill and the problem of the lost
money, and he assures the officer at Grantham that, just as his wit is
impoverished, so is his purse, which will remain so. He makes this
statement in the course of answering the officer's jibes one by one as
if they were ledger accounts and Cleveland had the responsibility of
making them balance. In response, for instance, to the officer's
former admonition "Be wise this side heaven," Cleveland says: "My

Wit shall be on what side Heaven you please, provided it ever be Antarctick to yours" (129). Ultimately, of course, Hill was not returned to the officer at Grantham; and Cleveland's editors found space for the mementos of the occasion. And they are interesting reading if only for the insight they give us into the exigencies of war and the conduct of gentlemen in arms. When shot and shell were silent, wit was abroad; and Cleveland and his adversary seem as intent on being successful in that style of battle as in any other. The unfortunate thing for the officer is that his opponent was the best of his kind, a man for whom wit was indeed a weapon which could be made to draw as much strength from the opposition as a successful battle of arms.

The last of Cleveland's English prose in the 1677 edition is the "Answer to the Newark-Summons," and it is the document most like the exchange with the officer. However, there is the significant distinction that there is little wit and no amusement in Cleveland's ardent refusal to surrender his garrison to Leslie, the Scot. As we know, King Charles himself finally intervened and ordered the garrison abandoned; but, until he spoke, Cleveland could only say, "when I received my Commission for the Government of this place, I annex'd my Life as a Label to my Trust" (172).

The answer is not curious only for its demonstration of Cleveland's loyalty or his bravery, though we can be reassured on both counts, but for its careful rhetorical structure and its studied form. We can be certain that the answer was not an unemotional production in response to an artificial situation: Cleveland was most definitely at Newark and was most definitely in certain danger of losing his life. Though he insists he did not read the letter which charged him to turn the garrison over to the Scots commander, it is not difficult to imagine that he was fully aware of the consequences of his action in refusing to submit to superior forces. Therefore, it is useful for us to observe that, when under such pressures and when confronted by an honest and profound emotional situation, Cleveland does not do as a modern would think he might and cast rhetorical forms to the winds. Instead, he is more cautious and more controlled in the use of rhetoric than ever.

The "Answer" is best compared on the count of rhetorical caution with the interchanges with the officer at Grantham. The rejoinders to the officer are marked by wit and brief sallies against the texture of the officer's statements, but the "Answer" avoids any taint of

specific response to specific charges, other than the overall response
to the charge of surrender. Instead, Cleveland develops a fulsome
metaphor which established Newark as a virgin blossom of the kingdom's glory defending herself against the immediate rape of bar-
baric invaders. The striking thing is that the language and the
strategy ring of Milton's *Comus,* while the opening sentence instantly recalls the "cloistered virtue" of *Areopagitica:*

> But that it argues a greater Courage to pass the Test of a Temptation
> uncorrupted, than with a timorous Vertue to decline the Trial, so jealous is
> this Maiden Garrison of sullying her Loyalty, that she had return'd your
> Summons without perusal. Which rebound of your Letter, as it were a
> laudable Coyness to preserve her Integrity; so it is the most compendious
> Answer to what you propound. For I hope you intend it rather as a Mode
> and Formality to preface your design, than with expectation of an Issue
> suitable to your Demands. You cannot imagine this untainted *Newark,*
> which hath so stoutly defended her Honour against several intended Rapes;
> should be so degenerous from her Virgin Glory as to admit the Courtship of
> either your Rival Nations. (169)

Newark remains a virgin only for a short time until the opening of
the reply is accomplished; although Cleveland relinquishes the
metaphor after having developed it this far—which is fulsome for
Cleveland—he does not abandon care in writing. The texture of the
rest of the reply is marked by the development of new metaphors
and by the attention paid to balance and grace in the writing of
individual sentences. Everywhere in the essay we observe smoothness and care in writing.

   "You may do well, Gentlemen," Cleveland warns, "to use your
Fortune modestly, and think not that God Almighty doth uphold
your Cause by reason of your Victories; perchance he fattens it with
present Success for a riper Destruction. For my part I had rather
embrace a Wrack floating upon a single Plank, than imbarque in
your Action with the fullest Sails to dance upon the Wings of Fortune" (171). The "new" ark to which he is clinging, and probably the
root of the metaphor and the pun in "imbarque," is quite clearly a
wreck, though he himself is unready to admit it. He admits he is
sorry to hear that the lands surrounding the garrison must support
the cost of the siege that the Scots level against him, but he also
feels that he must not let his sympathies compromise his honor:
"My Compassion to my Country must not make me a Parricide to
my Prince."

Such speculation, however, is qualified by Cleveland's suspicion that he may be either wrong or uninformed of the king's wishes. He declares himself to be completely unwilling to turn the garrison over to the Scots simply because it would be militarily prudent to do so. But he also declares that he will not be foolish and behave in a manner which would be contrary to the king's interest. Therefore, he closes his reply with the request for permission to send some of his own men to Oxford to ask whether the king "will wind up the Business in general, or leave every Commander to steer his own Course." Leslie, notwithstanding his profession of speed and impatience, seemingly chose to permit that request; and, when Cleveland was informed that the king's pleasure was that he should surrender, he did so immediately.

Cleveland's situation was tense; his options were few; and he must have been a desperate man. Yet his three-and-a-half page reply to a surrender demand looks as if it might have been written as a document to have been preserved through history, though history could hardly have been expected to take the seizure of Newark as having been anything but necessary and obvious. Cleveland spoke not as an actor in a drama which would be relived for all time but as a man who felt his situation to be so serious that he could not afford the slightest rhetorical lapse. Rhetoric and wit became more important as the situation grew more serious. Such, as we have seen, was also quite often the case with his poetry with relatively few exceptions. For Cleveland, the art of rhetoric was to become more rather than less important as the gravity of circumstances increased, and the gravity of circumstances at Newark could hardly have been much greater. The only conceivable event which might have tended to weight Cleveland's situation even more would have been the knowledge of the king's ultimate move: his sudden disappearance from Oxford and ultimate personal surrender to the Scots at Newark. Cleveland celebrated the sadness of this event in "The King's Disguise" a month after his reply to the officer at Newark. Both works are marked by a profound concern for metaphor and, in their different ways, for rhetorical purpose.

Surely one of Cleveland's most difficult personal situations was his imprisonment at the garrison at Yarmouth, the details of which are in part supplied in chapter 1 of this work, and supplementary information can be found in Berdan (39–46). In the worst of straits, having been imprisoned on suspicion of being someone who could do the state great harm, Cleveland wrote a most cautious and rhetorical appeal, sounding almost like a subject applying directly to his monarch. By November, 1655, of course, we might have good reason to think it only natural that Cromwell would be treated by most of his subjects as if he were the monarch indeed. And, though Cleveland must have been the victim of grave anxiety, little of it shows on the surface of the appeal.

He addresses Cromwell as "Your Highness," and treats him as if he were godlike, using the Plotinian images associated with omnipresence: "Rulers within the Circle of their Government have a Claim to that which is said of the Deity; they have their Center every where, and their Circumference no where. It is in this Confidence that I address to your Highness, knowing that no place in the Nation is so remote, as not to share in the Ubiquity of your Care; no Prison so close as to shut me up from partaking of your Influence" (142). The last of these words reminds us of "Upon the King's return from Scotland," in which we are told: "Kings travel by their beams and influence" (2), and we see that the rhetoric which suited King Charles is none too rarefied for Cromwell. We also see that, when he is in a pinch almost ten years after hostilities, Cleveland can use a rhetorical mode he associated with Royalty in addressing one who was once his most profound enemy.

Perhaps it is reading too much into the text, but it may well be that by using such a rhetorical posture, and by applying some of the same images which once were reserved for the king to the protector, Cleveland is giving some stylistic support to the claim he makes in this very letter that he is in "ten years Retirement from being engaged in the Differences of the State." Perhaps ten years have made a difference in his thinking, even if they were ten difficult years, with little income and considerable uncertainty.

We note one important feature of the appeal: it has all of the directness and all of the wit and metaphoric ingenuity of the reply to the officer's command to surrender at Newark. Cleveland is not any less sure of himself, nor is he any quicker to seize the main chance for personal safety. He is still his own man, and his mode of address to Cromwell is not a product of mere obsequiousness since we can see how directly he speaks to him and incriminates him in bringing him to his present pass. As Cleveland asserts in claiming his chief crime is poverty, not allegiance to the Royal party:

I only am the Prisoner who have no Acres to be my Hostage. Now, if my Poverty be Criminal (with Reverence be it spoken) I implead your Highness, whose Victorious Arms have reduced me to it, as Accessary to my Guilt. Let it suffice, my Lord, that the Calamity of the War hath made us poor, do not punish us for it. Who ever did Penance for being Ravished? Is it not enough that we are stripp'd so bare, but it must be made in order to a severer Lash? Must our Sores be engraven with our Wounds? Must we first be made Creeples, and then beaten with our own Crutches? Poverty, if it be a Fault 'tis its own Punishment, who pays more for it, pays use upon use. (143–44)

Thus Cleveland is not so groveling that he cannot put blame where it belongs: if Cromwell is responsible for his present affliction, then Cromwell can improve his condition.

Cleveland appeals to Cromwell's reputation as a vanquisher of kingdoms, as one who would remind posterity of what victory can mean. Likewise, he asks that Cromwell emulate the great and the victorious by being merciful. As he says, "The most renowned *Hero's* have ever with such Tenderness cherished their Captives, that their Swords did but cut out work for their Courtesies." "I hope your Highness, as you are the Rival of their Fame, will be no less of their Virtues. The Noblest Trophie that you can erect to your Honour is to raise the Afflicted; and since you have subdued all Opposition, it now remains that you attack your self, and with Acts of Mildness vanquish your Victory" (144). Cleveland reminds Cromwell that he has already shown considerable leniency to members of the Royalist party and that it would only be natural for him to extend that leniency to him.

But these appeals do not stand alone. Cleveland recommends his loyalty to King Charles as being one of his most important attributes. The "village Dogberrys" who imprisoned him in the first place indicated their fear that Cleveland was a Royalist; and, rather than deny it, Cleveland insists that his fidelity to his master would ensure his fidelity to Cromwell. The logic is not so careful as it might be, of course, since it can as easily be argued that the degree to which Cleveland was faithful to Prince Charles gives testament to the degree to which he would hold himself aloof from Cromwell. Yet, Cleveland says, "For the Service of his Majesty (if it be objected) I am so far from excusing it, that I am ready to alledge it in my Vindication. I cannot conceit that my Fidelity to my Prince should taint me in your Opinion, I should rather expect it should recommend me to your Favour. Had we not been Faithful to our King, we could not have given our selves to be so to your Highness; you had then trusted us *gratis,* whereas now we have our former Loyalty to vouch us."

Cleveland admits his loyalty, as he does his poverty, and points to them as being the causes of his imprisonment. At no time does Cleveland indicate he has lost faith with Charles who had been long dead; but he insists that his faithfulness does not interfere with his loyalty to the protector. He does, however, clearly distinguish between the two "charges" against him:

You see my Lord, how much I presume upon the Greatness of your Spirit, that dare prevent my Indictment with so frank a Confession, especially in this which I may so safely deny, that it is almost Arrogancy in me to own it: for the Truth is, I was not qualified enough to serve Him; all I could do was to bear a part in his Sufferings, and to give my self to be Crushed with his Fall. Thus my Charge is doubled; my Obedience to my Soveraign, and what is the Result of that, my want of Fortune. Now whatever reflection I have upon the former, I am a true Penitent for the latter. (145)

We can see without question that at no time does Cleveland falsify either his affections or his situation. He is a Royalist, and he is far from ashamed. He is poor, and he is regretful. But of his innocence he is quite certain. As he tells Cromwell, and as we at the moment must be willing to believe, he has made his peace with public affairs and has been in retirement. As I have already indicated, this particular conclusion has been attacked; and the suggestion has been made that Cleveland was active as an underground journalist during these years. However, the absolute honesty of this appeal to Cromwell's "Clemency" ought to give us pause for reflection. If Cleveland had been active, Cromwell's advisors would have known about him; and it is only reasonable to think that Cromwell would not have done what he did, namely, answer the appeal with release. But, of course, such speculation remains just that— uncertain, and nothing more than possible.

More important for the student of the prose is the personal rigor and honesty displayed by Cleveland in a very difficult situation. This honesty can serve as something of a guide for our examination of the uses of rhetoric and the purposes it serves, and it can help us determine whether Cleveland is engaged in broad general attack, as in his broadside barrages of the diurnals, or whether he is deeply involved and anxious to save his own person, as in his letters from Newark and Yarmouth. For Cleveland, since he was the Rhetoric Reader, rhetoric serves a useful and effective purpose. It is not the suspect art that it sometimes is in Milton's poetry. The interesting thing about Cleveland is that rhetoric is used most brilliantly and consistently, not when he wishes to be deceitful, but when he wishes to be most intense and most effective in personal statement. For the modern reader such a use of rhetoric is something of novelty, though it is merely upholding the ancient traditions which Cleveland so clearly respected.

Cleveland's prose is not only interesting, therefore, for the light it can afford for examing the poetry, but it is interesting in itself for its method. Again, the integrity of the prose and poetry, method and purpose, is something extraordinary and gives strength to the feeling that Cleveland's literary productions reflect his profoundest responses to life and circumstances. And, as artificial as they may seem to those of us who have forgotten the ancient uses and value of rhetoric and invention, they indicate a seriousness and responsiveness on the part of Cleveland which place him among the major writers of his time, though he will probably always be considered a minor writer.

CHAPTER 7

The Critical Reputation

I *The Eighteenth-Century Critics*

THOUGH the critical literature on Cleveland is not very extensive, the judgments which have been made about him have
usually been impassioned, long-lasting, and sometimes simply pre-
judiced. Certainly the foundation of all criticism of Cleveland has
been John Dryden's casual attribution to him of all that was undesir-
able in poetry. When Dryden held Cleveland up as an example he
was not interested in being fair or in being sympathetic. He characterized the Clevelandism as a "clownish kind of raillery"[1] in an effort
to demean his work. Whether or not Dryden could have been fair to
Cleveland had he wanted to is not easy to determine.

For one thing, Dryden did not have a reliable canon to guide him;
and we cannot be sympathetic to Cleveland unless we are willing to
look at all the work and see it in light of its times and its real
achievement. Dryden's political sympathies would not necessarily
have caused him to be unfair, even if he had thought of Cleveland as
a specifically political poet; his judgments were based on unsym-
pathetic readings of poems which do not stand up well alone. Like
Samuel Johnson, Dryden was none too sympathetic to the style
which Cleveland embraced, that of the inventive Metaphysical
mode. And neither Dryden nor Johnson, though they saw Cleveland as a "satyrist," concerned themselves with those aspects of his
style which pointed toward the more refined modes of the
eighteenth-century styles. When we assess the judgments of Dryden and Johnson, we can only suggest that they are representative
of the age, but they are by no means a full and adequate assessment
for us. Often what offended the eighteenth century is what gives us
pleasure today.

Dryden was simply establishing the critical judgment of his times
when he had Eugenius say: "The not observing this Rule is that

which the world has blam'd on the Satyrist *Cleveland;* to express a thing hard and unnaturally, is his new way of Elocution." He then continues by saying a poet may sometimes use a catachresis,

But to do this always, and never be able to write a line without it, though it may be admir'd by some few Pedants, will not pass upon those who know that wit is best convey'd to us in the most easie language; and is most to be admir'd when a great thought comes drest in words so commonly receiv'd that it is understood by the meanest apprehensions, as the best meat is the most easily digested: but we cannot read a verse of *Cleveland's* without making a face at it, as if every word were a Pill to swallow: he gives us many times a hard Nut to break our Teeth, without a Kernel for our pains. So that there is this difference betwixt his *Satyres* and Doctor Donns, That the one gives us deep thoughts in common language, though rough cadence; the other gives us common thoughts in abstruse words.[2]

Such an observation shows several things. One is that Dryden, or Eugenius, is establishing a rule for poetry which is similar to Wordsworth's plea for a poetry with more ordinary language. To be sure, Cleveland could have had no sympathy with such a rule; his delight was in finding the unusual word and using it brilliantly. In other words, the standard Eugenius is applying to Cleveland's poetry is one which Cleveland could never have survived. Another thing the comment shows us is that Eugenius is concerned more with thought than with language. His concern is for sentence and meaning rather than for the delight that Cleveland was anxious to provide his learned audience. Cleveland is not a poet of high meaning but one of effect. Eugenius is not concerned with that.

Samuel Johnson has very little to add to Eugenius's judgment. His own prejudice against the Metaphysical mode, no matter what its concerns, is well known. He attacked the "stiff twin compasses" of John Donne's "A Valediction Forbidding Mourning" with "it may be doubted whether absurdity or ingenuity has the better claim."[3] Furthermore, he attacked the metrical roughness of the style: "instead of writing poetry they only wrote verses, and very often such verses as stood the trial of the finger better than of the ear; for the modulation was so imperfect that they were only found to be verses by counting the syllables."[4] Much of this attack is based on an insistence on a decorum in poetry which was meaningless to Cleveland. These judgments, while possibly "right" for their age, cannot be considered adequate for our times. But, unfortunately, these judgments have endured and have really not been seriously challenged except by a few of the newer critics.

II   The Modern Critics

Some critics, like Geoffrey Walton, accept the views of the eighteenth-century critics. Walton has said, "Cleveland . . . is both decadent and stands at the end of a real cul-de-sac, virtuosity in words and technique for their own sake. He converts Metaphysical poetry into a brilliant intellectual game. It is pointless to ask with Johnson for realization of imagery or a consistent and unifying theme."[5] He adds, "Cleveland's main interest is ultimately not poetic at all: one might call it subfanciful."[6] It is difficult to know quite what Walton means by this statement, though it is not difficult to see that he recognizes at once that Cleveland will not measure up to the standards of Dryden and Johnson.

Other critics, like George Williamson, can find individual aspects of the poet's work to praise; but in the end they find him not very successful. In Williamson's essay on the strong line, for instance, he praises Cleveland for the same quality for which Cleveland's earliest editors, Lake and Drake, praised his ability to produce the strong line. Williamson concludes that Cleveland is "a strong-lined poet who in reality, has sunk into the defects of his qualities."[7] In other words Cleveland's ingenuity and wit undermined his achievement in the end. Such a judgment, again, is based on a reading of only some of the poems and for essentially one quality of them.

A critic who is more formidable because he is more intensive in his discussion of Cleveland is A. Alvarez, but his judgment coincides with Williamson's. In Alvarez's discussion of Cleveland in his chapter "The Game of Wit and the Corruption of the Style," he suggests that the university coterie for which Cleveland wrote may not have been either so small or so exclusive as it is sometimes thought, for the vocabulary Cleveland used was easily available to most university people. Even in discussing Cleveland's poem on Edward King, Alvarez considers that there is a possibility that the rhetoric may be inflated for a purpose, though he remains skeptical about that: "Perhaps there is supposed to be a parallel between the excessiveness of his grief and the galvanic leaps and bounds of his wit. But even if there were, the concept of wit has clearly altered a good deal since the earlier days of the School of Donne. Instead of being an individual power by which the poet discriminates and synthesizes his material, wit has become a simple mechanism for turning out novel and learned periphrases."[8] Alvarez is right in his assessment of the changes in wit represented by Cleveland in his poem on King, but he may not be right in dismissing the connection between his stylistic excess and that of his grief.

Alvarez is sensitive to Cleveland's wit, but he dismisses it as "simply trying to be amusing, or 'witty' in the modern sense." He describes some poems as being nothing but "strings of dapper jokes and epigrams." And his conclusion is that "Poetry for Cleveland and his followers was a game of wit, whose counters were words and whose rules were the frame of reference to University learning."[9]

Even K. K. Ruthven, who in his study of the conceit sets aside a portion of a chapter to discuss the Clevelandism, remarks that "Cleveland's formula was one of erudite whimsicality verging on the grotesque. As a decadent (in the strictly literary sense of the word) he made the Metaphysical style the subject of his poetry and treated each poem as an occasion for a display of wit. Metaphysical conceits are therefore at their most vulnerable in the Clevelandism, where emotion is supplanted by intellect and everything is directed to the display of intellectual brilliance."[10] Ruthven does, however, point out the fact that the Clevelandism is based on the use of catachresis but that the very term was itself loaded when applied to Cleveland: it meant an unacceptable misuse of language.

The harshest criticism of Cleveland's work has been reserved for his lyric poetry. Of late, his satire has been given some growing recognition. C. V. Wedgwood says, for instance, that Cleveland's satirical verse is "the most bitter that the Civil War produced";[11] and her admiration for Cleveland is considerable and her criticism well detailed. She concludes by asserting that "He was the sharpest and most insistently topical of the Cavaliers."[12] Ruth Nevo is even more outspoken when she declares, "political verse as such comes of age with the work of John Cleveland in the 1640's."[13] She is also aware that Cleveland owed a great deal to rhetorical invention. As she says, "*Upon the King's Return from Scotland, 1641*, one of Cleveland's earliest attempts at political poetry, consists of a series of violent conceits, drawn from various 'places of invention,' to illustrate the idea of the inseparability of King and State."[14] Mrs. Nevo sees the violence of the conceits as one of the most important achievements of Cleveland's style: "Saintsbury has suggested that Cleveland caricatured, or near-burlesqued, the metaphysical manner. But in the light of the whole body of seventeenth century political verse, and his influence upon Butler, it would be more appropriate to see in the oddities of his style a first attempt to solve the central problem of decorum which faced the partisan writer. He must find, or invent, a style which will express both adulation and animus. It is Cleveland's wit, his catachresis, his contorted conceit, which serves as a unifying medium between the two poles."[15] Such views seem more responsive to the real character of Cleveland's work than those views held by earlier critics. Mrs. Nevo is accurate in citing the uses of decorum, in spotting the reliance on rhetorical invention, and in linking the work with the age.

Of course, the best of the modern critics is probably Harry Levin, but his views—in a single article published in 1934—are predictably in agreement with the main lines of eighteenth-century criticism. My own readings of the poems differ from his more frequently than not, but one of the reasons is simply that I have had access to a better text. Levin is not so much concerned about the rhetorical character of the verse, its usefulness as satire, and he is not so sympathetic a reader of Cleveland as he says he is; but Levin is valuable for a discussion of the criticism and for a close critical reading of the poems. His essay laments the fact that, when the reputations of the Metaphysical poets were revived, Cleveland's was not among them. He puts it squarely: "There are some writers who may not be mentioned without apology, and John Cleveland is definitely in that category. For about twenty-five years, no English poet was so strenuously cultivated; for the two hundred and fifty years between that time and this, none has been so pointedly ignored."[16] Levin's concern is with the conceit in Cleveland's hands; and, though he does not stem the tide of adverse criticism, he does offer some acute interpretations of lines and some valuable ways of looking at the poetry.

III   *The Modern Editors*

No discussion of the criticism of Cleveland's work is complete without mentioning the work of John Berdan, George Saintsbury, and Brian Morris and Eleanor Withington, the superb modern editors. Berdan was the first editor in the twentieth century. His life of Cleveland is still standard, though he is not so acute a critic that his sympathies with Cleveland could be kept fully under control. Often his sympathetic judgments would not be terribly convincing for someone whose views were different from his own. Berdan is, then, not really at his best as a critic, though he argues for a better and more sympathetic reading of all the poetry. Some of his discussions are valuable even for a modern reader.

George Saintsbury also edited the poems a few years after Berdan's edition was printed. Saintsbury was rather high-handed in his treatment of Berdan because Berdan was an American, and Berdan had "scooped" him by getting his edition into print before Saintsbury—then certainly the most eminent and imposing scholar of the language in England. Whenever he can, Saintsbury corrects Berdan, usually in a manner designed to be abusive; and his treatment of Cleveland is typical. He accepts the views of Dryden and Johnson and takes every opportunity to compare Cleveland with Dryden in order to elevate Dryden and denigrate Cleveland. He asserts that Cleveland was a failure as a poet; but because he was not much of a poet, he was not much of a failure. Saintsbury laments more the failure of Cleveland as a satirist, asserting that at least he had some talent in that direction.

Saintsbury is important for his notes to the poems, but he is not important for his critical introduction except insofar as the introduction offers in brief a view of the prevailing hostile critical mood. This mood demanded propriety and stood for nothing less. Thus, Saintsbury's views are curious, but marked by essentially the same demands and the same limitations of the eighteenth-century critics.

Morris and Withington, on the other hand, have a highly valuable critical introduction to their edition. They cite the standard critical objections which had characterized all Cleveland criticism: the excessive wit, the use of catachresis, the topicality, the failure to integrate and develop images and themes, and the reliance on highly technical language. In many cases they do not disagree with the main lines of criticism, but they do offer some fresh reading of poems in an effort to develop a new perspective. By and large, their readings are full, independent, and reliable.

IV *A Modern Reassessment*

I have tried to continue what I feel has been begun by the Morris and Withington edition: a modern reassessment of Cleveland's work. My feeling is that Cleveland has suffered because of the critical attitudes of succeeding ages and not because of a failure of his own talent. Once the work has been done to reconstruct the

historical, political, and religious circumstances which figure so pro-
foundly in the poems, we are in a better position to see the full
effect of them. My readings of the poems have concentrated on
establishing a full historical context in which to regard Cleveland's
work; for, without that context, his work is very likely to be unfairly
treated.

Moreover, I have emphasized the nature of Cleveland's commitment to rhetoric as it was understood in his age. Later times have
not appreciated rhetorical poetry, but Cleveland's time certainly
held it in esteem. Since we do not highly value rhetoric in our time
(Milton records it as falling out of favor) and since we do not study
rhetoric in anything like the manner the seventeenth-century
schoolboy would have studied it, we are naturally troubled by some
of the effects Cleveland achieves. As the most powerful public poet
of his day, Cleveland had to make complete use of rhetoric in his
poetry. He had all the qualifications he could have needed, and his
own university recognized him as a master of rhetoric even before
he became famous in the nation at large.

To master rhetoric is, in short, to master the materials which have
an effect on the psychology of an audience. It is to be aware of the
expectations, the norms, the permissible decorum of an audience
and to use that knowledge to change the audience's concept of a
subject. Cleveland used his rhetorical skills to attack and belittle
political and religious opponents. But he used them, too, to express
his own deeper feelings since he saw in the extremity of his rhetorical invention an analogy for the extremity of his emotional commitment. For the rhetorician, wit was a surgical instrument which laid
bare not only its victim but sometimes the rhetorician's deepest
feelings.

Regarding Cleveland as a master of rhetoric and admitting the
prejudices of successive ages against rhetoric mixed with poetry
should help us understand why it is difficult to appreciate some of
his work. Reviving Cleveland is probably a job similar to that of
reviving the Mannerist painters, whose incompetence has been
taken for granted until our own century. Recent art historians began
to see that their work was not technically deficient but basically
rhetorical in nature: it was designed to affect a viewer in a way he
might not like but could not ignore.

The purposes of Cleveland's energy, inventiveness, audacity, and
simple shock are clearly of this order. He does not lose control of his

poems, as careful examination of the prosody shows. Criticism which asserts Cleveland had no control of his materials seems unwarranted by careful reading of the poems and prose. Cleveland knew what he was doing, and we cannot help but admire his brilliance. He remains one of the most inventive lyricists of his time— and of the style which virtually ended with him. And perhaps more important for the post-Romantic reader, Cleveland must be considered an absolute master of what we have come to call the English satire. His genius as a satirist in his own day had no peer. In terms of the history of English literature, Cleveland must be considered original, brilliant, and among the first rank of satirists in the language.

Notes and References

Preface

1. John Dryden, *Works,* ed. Walter Scott and rev. George Saintsbury (1808, London 1882–93), XV, 287.

Chapter One

1. The standard life is, and will be for some time, still the introduction to John M. Berdan's *Poems of John Cleveland* (New Haven, 1903). My account depends on Berdan heavily, though it is wise also to see Brian Morris and Eleanor Withington, *The Poems of John Cleveland* (Oxford, 1967), for their summary life and for their inclusion of "four contemporary accounts" of Cleveland's life: from Thomas Fuller's *Worthies,* Edward Phillips (Milton's nephew) from *Theatrum Poetarum,* Aubrey's *Brief Lives,* and a funeral elegy written (before Cleveland died) by "S. H." See the Selected Bibliography for additional lives. See also Samuel Vogt Gapp, "Notes on John Cleveland," Publication of the Modern Languages Association, 46 (1931), 1075–86.

2. For additional information, see John L. Kimmey, "John Cleveland, His Poetry and Influence" (Ph.D. diss. Columbia University, 1955). Kimmey discusses Thomas Cleveland's difficulties with Parliament.

3. The most interesting source for information about life at Christ's during the years Cleveland was there is William Riley Parker, *Milton: a Biography,* 2 vols. (Oxford, 1968), I, 23–115. The notes in vol. II also include many important details.

4. *Clievelandi Vindiciae,* ed. John Lake and Samuel Drake (London, 1677), sig. A6^r.

5. *Ibid.,* sig. A6^v.

6. S. V. Gapp, *op. cit.,* p. 1078.

7. *Clievelandi Vindiciae,* sig. A7^r.

8. Berdan, p. 35.

9. *Ibid.,* p. 39.

10. *Ibid.,* pp. 39–40.

11. David Underdown, *Royalist Conspiracy in England: 1649–1660* (New Haven, 1960), pp. 164–65.

12. *Ibid.,* p. 166.

13. Berdan, pp. 41–42.

14. Morris and Withington, p. xxi, as reprinted from John Aubrey, *Brief Lives*, 2 vols., ed., Andrew Clark (Oxford, 1898), I, 174–75. Aubrey wrote his lives sometime in the 1680s.

Chapter Two

1. *Of Dramatick Poesie*, ed. James T. Boulton (Oxford, 1964), p. 38.
2. *Lives of the English Poets*, ed. George Birkbeck Hill, 3 vols. (1905; reprinted., New York, 1967), I, 27.
3. *Of Dramatick Poesie*, p. 59.
4. See Fuller's life in Morris and Withington, p. xix.

Chapter Three

1. James Sutherland reinforces this point in "Anne Greene and the Oxford Poets," in *The Augustan Milieu: Essays presented to Louis A. Landa*, ed. Henry Knight Miller, Erich Rothstein, and G. S. Rousseau (Oxford, 1970), p. 3.
2. George Kitchin, *A Survey of Burlesque and Parody in English* (London, 1941), p. 85.

Chapter Four

1. Ruth Nevo, *The Dial of Virtue* (Princeton, 1963), p. 3.
2. George Saintsbury, ed., *Minor Poets of the Caroline Period*, 3 vols. (Oxford, 1905–1921), III, 68n.
3. See Ursula M. Cowgill, "The People of York: 1538–1812," *Scientific American* 222 (1970), 104–12.
4. Saintsbury, III, 62n.
5. Of this comparison, C. V. Wedgwood has this to say: "Cleveland, the most dexterous poet to deal in political verse, in a poem on Prince Rupert used the heightened classical allusions so common in the elegant poems of the 1630's. But this time, provided we take the lines, as Cleveland certainly meant them to be taken, with a certain humour, his classical comparison is not (as with Carew or Townshend) merely ornamental; it is lavishly flattering, but also ingeniously apt. Cleveland was describing the notorious daring of the prince and his almost equally notorious good luck: though he was always in the hottest of the battle, he had never yet been wounded. Cleveland therefore compared him to Perseus, son of Danae, begotten by Jupiter in a shower of gold," *Poetry and Politics Under the Stuarts* (Cambridge, 1960), p. 79. Miss Wedgwood is quite right, I think, in assuming that a considerable amount of humor is implicit in these lines, just as there is in the section devoted to Boy and his malignant leg. Still, however, the problems with the imagery remain.
6. See their discussion in *Poems*, pp. lxv ff. They treat this poem as fundamentally satirical and point up what they feel is Cleveland's frustration expressed in his ambivalent attitudes toward the king: "On the one

hand wè are commanded to regard the King's disguise as libellous, blasphemous, ridiculous . . . on the other Charles's 'ruines' prove 'a religious house'."

7. Morris and Withington cite this in their notes, p. 86.

8. See Thomas B. Dewey, "Some 'Careless' Seventeenth-Century Rhymes," *Bulletin of the New York Public Library* 69 (1965), 143–52.

Chapter Five

1. See Morris and Withington, pp. lviii–lix and p. 91; John Peter, *Complaint and Satire in Early English Literature* (Oxford, 1956), p. 119.

2. C. V. Wedgwood, *Poetry and Politics Under the Stuarts* (Cambridge, 1960), pp. 2, 85.

3. Berdan provides a thumbnail sketch of the situation (pp. 117–18) as well as the version of the oath I quote, and Godfrey Davies summarizes some of the chief points conveniently in *The Early Stuarts, 1603–1660* (Oxford, 1959), pp. 68–99.

4. Saintsbury, p. 43n. William P. Williams in "The Childrens Threes" in *American Notes and Queries* 9 (1971), 83–84 suggests a connection with a latin tag, *jus trium liberorum,* a phrase that came "to stand for the most common, and hence, least effective sort of political or official reward." Jeremy Taylor uses the phrase in *The Liberty of Prophesying* (London, 1647) published the same year as Cleveland's first book of poems.

5. See William Ames, *A Marrow of Sacred Divinity* (London, 1641). The first twenty-five pages are Ramist "divisions" or dichotomies of the text of the book, which is itself a Christian Doctrine on the order of Milton's *De Doctrina Christiana.*

6. See "Heraldic Conceits" in K. K. Ruthven, *The Conceit* (London, 1969), pp. 31f.

7. See Godfrey Davies, pp. 190–95, for a summary of events.

8. As Morris and Withington call it in their introduction, p. lxiii.

9. See Shakespeare, *Henry V,* II. iii. 38ff.

10. See Morris and Withington's note, p. 104.

11. See Davies, p. 106 and notes.

Chapter Six

1. See "Mixed Assembly," line 98. It means simply to be divided up the middle, as on a coat of arms, so that the field can show through.

Chapter Seven

1. *Of Dramatick Poesy,* ed. James T. Boulton (Oxford, 1964), p. 38.

2. *Ibid.,* p. 59.

3. *Lives of the English Poets,* ed. George Birkbeck Hill, 3 vols. (Oxford, 1905), I, 34.

4. *Ibid.,* p. 19.

5. Geoffrey Walton, *Metaphysical to Augustan* (London, 1955), p. 64.

6. *Ibid.*, p. 65.

7. See Ruth Wallerstein, *Studies in Seventeenth-Century Poetic* (Madison, 1961), pp. 72ff. Also see John L. Kimmey's doctoral dissertation, cited in Note 2, chapter 1. The original source for the revival of interest in the subject is George Williamson, "Strong Lines," *English Studies* 18 (1936), 152–59, reprinted in Williamson's *Seventeenth Century Contexts* (Chicago, 1969), pp. 120–31. The line I quote is from this edition, p. 128.

8. George Williamson, *The School of Donne* (New York, 1961, 1967), p. 103.

9. *Ibid.*, p. 104.

10. K. K. Ruthven, *The Conceit* (London, 1969), p. 50.

11. C. V. Wedgwood, *Poetry and Politics Under the Stuarts* (Cambridge, 1960), p. 2. See also her more popular piece, "A Metaphysical Satirist," in *The Listener* 59 (May 8, 1958), 769–71.

12. *Ibid.*, pp. 85–86.

13. Ruth Nevo, *The Dial of Virtue* (Princeton, 1963), p. 3.

14. *Ibid.*, p. 42.

15. *Ibid.*, p. 44.

16. Harry Levin, "John Cleveland and the Conceit," *Criterion* 14 (1934) 40.

Selected Bibliography

PRIMARY SOURCES

1. *Seventeenth-century editions (selected)*
   See Morris and Withington, listed in "Modern Editions" below, for complete details on these editions and on editions of individual poems.

The Character of a London-Driurnall, with several select Poems by the same Author. London, 1647. Eight printings, six editions.

Poems, by J. C., With Additions. London, 1651. Five editions.

Poems, by J. C., With Additions never before Printed. London, 1653. Two editions, with an edition each in 1656 and 1657.

Poems, Characters, and Letters. By J. C. With Additions never before Printed. London, 1658. Two editions.

J. Cleaveland Revived. London: Nathaniel Brook, 1659. With an edition each in 1660, 1662, and 1668.

Poems. By John Cleavland. With Additions never before Printed. London, 1659. With editions by different printers in 1661, 1662, 1665, and 1669.

Clievelandi Vindiciae, or Clieveland's Genuine Poems, Orations, Epistles, etc. London, 1677. Three issues that year. This is usually considered the most reliable edition, edited by Bishop Lake and Samuel Drake.

The Works of Mr. John Cleveland. London, 1687. Also reprinted in 1699 and 1742.

2. *Modern Editions*

The Poems of John Cleveland. Edited by John M. Berdan. New Haven: Yale University Press, 1903, 1911. Has the best life as well as some useful appendixes.

John Cleveland, in *Minor Poets of the Caroline Period.* Edited by George Saintsbury. Vol. III. Oxford: Clarendon Press, 1921.

The Poems of John Cleveland. Edited by Brian Morris and Eleanor Withington. Oxford: Clarendon Press, 1967. This is the standard edition.

SECONDARY SOURCES

DRYDEN, JOHN. *Of Dramatick Poesie.* Edited by James T. Boulton. Oxford: Oxford University Press. 1964. Contains the earliest definition of the Clevelandism.

JOHNSON, SAMUEL. *Lives of the English Poets*. Edited by George Birkbeck Hill. 3 vols. Oxford: Oxford University Press, 1905. See Volume I, *Life of Cowley*.

ALVAREZ, A. *The School of Donne*. New York: New American Library, 1961, 1967. See "The Game of Wit and the Corruption of the Style." Valuable study.

DEWEY, THOMAS B. "Some Careless Seventeenth-Century Rhymes. *Bulletin of the New York Public Library* 69 (1965), 143–52. Discusses contemporary pronunciation and its relationship to some apparently careless rhymes in the period.

GAPP, SAMUEL VOGT. "Notes on John Cleveland." *PMLA*, 46 (1931), 1075–86. This article discusses the likelihood that Cleveland was working for the underground press from the time of his surrender at Newark to the time of his death in 1658. It is highly speculative, but accepted on Gapp's research by the editors of the *Cambridge Bibliography of English Literature*.

GOSSE, EDMUND. "The Reaction." In *From Shakespeare to Pope*. New York: Dodd Mead & Company, 1896. In passing, Gosse summed up his generation's unconcern for Cleveland.

KIMMEY, JOHN L. "John Cleveland and the Satiric Couplet in the Restoration." *Philological Quarterly* 37 (1958), 410–23. Discusses the influences on Dryden and others of the techniques Cleveland developed for his own satires.

LEVIN, HARRY. "John Cleveland and the Conceit." *Criterion* 14 (1934), 40–53. Remains one of the clearest discussions of Cleveland's style.

MORRIS, BRIAN. "Satire from Donne to Marvell." *Metaphysical Poetry*. Stratford-Upon-Avon-Studies 11. London: Edward Arnold, 1970. Morris sees Cleveland in relationship to the growth of satire. Good for a general grasp of the growth of the mode and Cleveland's role in that growth.

SUTHERLAND, JAMES. "Anne Greene and the Oxford Poets." In *The Augustan Milieu: Essays present to Louis A. Landa*, Edited by Henry Knight Miller, Eric Rothstein, G. S. Rousseau. Oxford: Oxford University Press, 1970. Cleveland is treated in the opening section as one of the "University wits." Good for background on the methods of university trained poets writing for a university audience.

WEDGWOOD, C. V. "A Metaphysical Satirist," *The Listener* 59 (1958), 769–71. Popular treatment, but quite interesting. States plainly the claims Cleveland has for being original and influential in the mode of satire.

Index